A
Staffordshire
Christmas

A
Staffordshire
Christmas

Compiled by Robin Pearson

ALAN SUTTON

First published in the United Kingdom in 1993 by
Alan Sutton Publishing Limited · Phoenix Mill · Far Thrupp
Stroud · Gloucestershire

First published in the United States of America in 1993 by
Alan Sutton Publishing Inc · 83 Washington Street
Dover · NH 03820

British Library Cataloguing in Publication Data

A catalogue record for this book is available
from the British Library.

ISBN 0-7509-0000-0

Library of Congress Cataloging in Publication Data
applied for

Jacket illustration: Selling Christmas Trees *by D.J. Jacobson;*
Gavin Graham Gallery (courtesy of The Bridgeman Art Library,
London).

Typeset in Garamond 12/13.
Typesetting and origination by
Alan Sutton Publishing Limited.
Printed in Great Britain by
Redwood Books, Trowbridge, Wiltshire.

Contents

A Staffordshire Christmas

A Staffordshire Christmas

A Staffordshire Christmas

Lichfield's statue of Hanley born Edward John Smith, the *Titanic* captain

Customs Past and Present

CHARLES HENRY POOLE

Many of his recollections of Staffordshire customs, superstitions and legends were originally published by Charles Henry Poole as newspaper articles but were eventually produced in book form in 1886. He also compiled a glossary of Staffordshire dialect as well as jointly editing a book about the county's poets.

CHRISTMAS AND NEW YEAR'S DAY

At Christmas be merry and thankful withal,
And feast thy poor neighbours, the great and the small.

Tusser

The Season of the Nativity is now no longer marked by that hospitality which characterized its observance among our forefathers. In many an ancient hall of this shire, the Squire would assemble all his tenants and neighbours at daybreak. The strongest beer in the cellar was broached, and the horns went plentifully about with toast, sugar, nutmeg, and good Cheshire cheese. Every one ate heartily, and every one was welcome. The Wassail-bowl, the yule-log, the lord of misrule, together with many other customs of ancient days, made our 'Merrie Englande' conspicuous among the nations of Europe

for its observance of Christmastide; the decking of churches and houses with holly and other evergreens, and invitations to family parties, together with the issue of so-called Christmas numbers, published months before this blessed festival dawns, and, sad to say, having scarcely any allusion to it, are the only reminders of this gladsome season. However, my purpose is to present some of those ancient customs which once prevailed.

The 'Waits,' whose music now is heard only at this festive season, are the descendants of the songsters who lived in the musical times of England, and who now play by night for two or three weeks before Christmas. In their palmier days even they came in for a share of abuse, for in the *Ship of Fools*, is a description of the 'wanderers' whose crime was so great –

'That by no means can they abide, ne dwell,
Within their houses, but out they need must go,' &c.

Barclay, in another passage, gives vent to his wrath, the winter minstrels coming in for a share of it:

'But yet moreover these *fools*, are so unwise,
That in cold winter they use the same madness;
When all the houses are lade with snow and ice,
O! madmen amased, unstable and witless!
What pleasure take you in this your foolishness,
What joy have ye to wander thus by night,
Save that ill doers, always hate the light?'

As time went on, destroying antiquated customs, they, with poetry, lost their honours and abiding place, and also their 'vested rights' to serenade the fair, and to assist them through their courtships. A relic of the Timbril-Waits lingered in Staffordshire, as appears from a correspondent who recently contributed to the 'Local Notes and Queries' of the

The Smith family of Basin Cottages, Armitage Road, Rugeley,
about to enjoy their 1910 Christmas pig roast

Wolverhampton Chronicle, although he did not say in what part
of the County he observed the custom.

'It was,' he says, 'usual fifty years ago, and continued for
many years after that time, for working boys, during the
four or five weeks before Christmas, to join in parties of
about four, five, six, or seven, to start out each weekday
morning at about four or five o'clock, with tin kettles or
old iron pans, and to beat them as hard as they could
along the streets. The more noise they made the better it
was considered, as their object was to awaken the
sleepers in order that they might arise early to begin
work. Many boys who were awakened by the earliest "tin
kettlers," as they were called, formed themselves into
parties and went through a few streets, "beating up." If

the old watchmen had not left their rounds they sometimes dispersed these inharmonious musicians, but many working men considered the custom a very valuable one. I do not know how early, or rather, how much earlier than my own recollection this "tin kettling" began.'

'Wassailing' was publicly observed at Lichfield, the choir of the Cathedral calling upon the inhabitants with a cup, and asking either for money or drink. The origin of this custom is to be found in the visit of Hengist and Horsa, at the instigation of Vortigern; the British chief became enamoured with Rowena, the beautiful niece of Hengist. At a feast given by Hengist in honour of Vortigern, Rowena presented a cup of spiced wine to the aged Prince, and with smiles addressed these words to him – 'Waes-heal,' to which he replied 'Drinc-heal.' Robert of Gloucester narrates the event which has been paraphrased thus:

> 'Health, my Lord King!' the sweet Rowena said,
> 'Health!' cried the chieftain to the Saxon maid;
> Then gaily rose, and mid the concourse wide;
> Kissed her hale lips, and placed her by his side.
> At the soft scene such gentle thoughts abound,
> That healths and kisses 'mongst the guests went round:
> From this the social custom took its rise,
> We still retain, and still must keep the prize.

Waes-heal, from this period, became the name of drinking cups of the Saxons in their feasts. Wessell, Wassal, Wassell, Wassel, Washaile, Wassail Bowls, are therefore only altered modes of spelling the ancient Waes-heal or Wish-health Bowls. Drinking parties were called Wassels – the jovial partakers – Wassalers or Wassailers. The custom of Wassail

was anciently observed in the monasteries. Placed, in front of the Abbot, was the 'Poculum Caritatis,' and from it the superior drank to all, and then passed it on to the remainder of his brethren. The corporation feasts of London still preserve the custom, as also the Universities, which is a reminder of the ancient merrie times. A double-handed flagon, full of mulled wine, is handed to the master; he drinks standing to the general health, as announced by the toast-master; and then passes it to his left hand neighbour, who drinks standing to his next neighbour, who remains standing, and so on it goes, until all have drunk. At Lichfield, too, at dinners given by the mayor, or at any public feast of the corporation, the first toast proposed is that of the Queen, followed by that of the Weale and Worship, both of which are drunk out of a massive silver cup, holding three or four quarts, which was presented to the corporation in 1606 by Elias Ashmole. The ceremony is as follows: – The mayor drinks first, and on his rising, the persons on his right and left also rise; he then hands the cup to the one on his right hand, when the one next to him rises, the one on the left of the mayor still standing; then the cup is passed across the table to him, when his left hand neighbour rises; so that there are always three standing at the same time, one next to the person who drinks, and one opposite to him. At the annual Vinis, or feast of the mock corporation of Hanley, formerly the initiation of each member consisted in his swearing fealty to the body, and drinking a yard of wine, *i.e.*, a pint of port or sherry, from a glass one yard in length. Ward, too, in his *Borough of Stoke-upon-Trent, etc.,* 1843, gives a list of the seventy gentlemen assembled at the civic feast, whose names are registered in the Corporation Book, and adds –

The test of admission to the freedom of this convivial corporation, was the drinking off a yard-length glass of

ale at a single draught, no very trifling infliction on a temperate candidate. Strong ale was mostly in vogue at the parties of those early days and after ample libations offered to Sir John Barleycorn, large bowls of punch crowned the convivial board, wine being introduced but sparingly.

*   *   *

MORRICE AND HOBBY-HORSE DANCING

Most antiquaries are of opinion that the old English morrice dance, so great a favourite in this country in the sixteenth century, was derived through Spain from the Moors; and that its name in Spanish (Morisco) a Moor, was taken from this circumstance. It has been supposed to have been originally identified with the fandango. It was certainly popular in France as early as the fifteenth century, under the name of Morisque, which is an intermediate step between the Spanish Morisco and the English Morris or Morrice.

The morrice dance became a popular pastime of the English in the early years of the sixteenth century, towards the close of the reign of Henry VII, and the commencement of that of his successor, bluff King Hal. We find it to have been much favoured in Staffordshire and Mid-England generally, where it grew to form a prominent part in the Christmas and May Festivals.

A tract of the time of Charles I, entitled 'Mythomistes,' speaks of 'The best taught country morrice dancer, with all his bells and napkins,' as being sometimes employed at Christmas.

Hobby-Horsing is mentioned by Dr Plot as having existed in the town of Abbots' Bromley within the memory of many persons alive at the period when he wrote. It was a sort of

amusement which the inhabitants celebrated at Christmas, on New Year's Day, and Twelfth Day. On these occasions a person danced through the principal street, carrying between his legs the figure of a horse composed of thin boards; in his hands he held a bow and arrow which, passing through a hole in the bow, and stopping on a shoulder in it, made a sort of snapping noise as he drew it to and fro, keeping time with the music. Five or six other individuals danced along with this person, each carrying on his shoulder six reindeers' heads, three of them painted white, and three red, with the arms of the chief families, who had at different times been proprietors of the manor, painted on the *palms* of them. To this hobby-horse dance, there also belonged a pot, which was kept by turns by four or five of the chief men of the town, whom they called *reeves*, who provided cake and ale to put into this pot. All the people who had any kindness for the good interest of the

A 1982 heavy snowfall ices up canal boats at Fradley Junction

institution of the sport, gave a penny apiece for themselves and families, and so strangers too, that came to see it, with which money the charge of the cakes and ale being defrayed, they not only repaired their church, but kept their poor too: which charges are not now perhaps so cheerfully borne. This practice seems to have existed at other places in this Shire; for we find hobby-horse money frequently mentioned in the old parish books, both of Stafford and Seighford. Sir Simon Degge says in his work that this money was appropriated to repair the Church of Stafford, and that the man who contributed most to the hobby-horse was considered as possessing most credit, so that each townsman strove to improve his interest, as he remembered it was accounted for at Christmas.

*   *   *

CURIOUS CHARITABLE CUSTOMS

> Who largely gives with willing hand,
> Or quickly gives with liberal heart;
> His fame shall spread throughout the land,
> His memory thence shall ne'er depart.

At Aldridge it was customary for the vicar to give a dinner every Christmas Day to each individual, young and old, residing in the parish. The origin of this curious practice is now wholly unknown. Within these few years it has been discontinued, writes Nightingale, the clergyman paying 6*d*. to every householder to regale his family at home. At Great Barr, the rector also on this day was accustomed to give each parishioner, great and small, that came to his house, as much bread, beef, mustard, and vinegar, as they could eat. Latterly, however, money was given instead. At Stafford, too, there is an ancient payment made by the chamberlain of the

corporation, of an annual sum of money at Christmas, generally six shillings, for the purchasing of plums, to be distributed among the inhabitants of certain old houses in the liberty of Forebridge. The origin of this payment is ascribed by general reputation to the bounty of some individual who heard some poor children complaining that they had no plums for a pudding; and it is reported that he counted the houses then in the place, and made provisions for the supply of a pound of plums to each house. The money received is laid out in plums, which are divided into equal quantities and made up into parcels, one for each of the fifteen or sixteen in number, entitled by the established usage to receive a portion, without reference to the circumstances of the inhabitants.

On Christmas Day: Hymn

CHARLES COTTON

Although famous as a seventeenth–century poet and translator of the French essayist Montaigne, Charles Cotton will always be remembered for his friendship with fellow Staffordshire writer, Izaak Walton. In 1676 he added a treatise on fly-fishing to the fifth edition of The Compleat Angler.

Rise, happy mortals, from your sleep,
Bright Phosphor now begins to peep,
In such apparel as ne'er drest
The proudest day-break of the East!
   Death's sable curtain 'gins disperse,
     And now the blessed morn appears,
       Which has long'd and pray'd for him
     So many centuries of years,
       To defray th' arrears of sin.
   Now through the joyful universe
     Beams of mercy and of love
     Shoot forth comfort from above,
   And choirs of angels do proclaim
   The holy Jesus' blessed name.

Rise, shepherds, leave your flocks, and run;
The soul's great Shepherd now is come!
Oh! wing your tardy feet, and fly
To greet this dawning majesty:
   Heaven's messenger, in tidings bless'd,
     Invites you to the sacred place,
       Where the blessed Babe of joy,
       Wrapp'd in his holy Father's grace,
       Comes the serpent to destroy,
   That lurks in ev'ry human breast.
       To Judah's Beth'lem turn your feet,
       There you shall salvation meet;
     There, in a homely manger hurl'd,
     Lies the Messias of the world.

Riding upon the morning's wings,
The joyful air salvation sings,
'Peace upon Earth, tow'rds men good will,'
Echoes from ev'ry vale and hill;

A perfect place for a snowball fight

For why, the Prince of Peace is come,
  The glorious Infant, who this morn
    (By a strange mysterious birth)
  Is of his virgin mother born,
    To redeem the seed of Earth
From foul rebellious heavy doom.
    Travel, magi of the East,
    To adore this sacred Guest;
  And offer up (with reverence)
  Your gold, your myrrh, and frankincense.

At th' teeming of this blessed womb
All nature is one joy become;
The fire, the earth, the sea, and air,
The great salvation to declare:
    The mountains skip with joy's excess,
    The ocean's briny billows swell
      O'er the surface of their lands,
    And at this sacred miracle
      Floods do clap their liquid hands,
Joy's inundation to express:
      Babes spring in the narrow rooms
      Of their tender mothers' wombs,
    And all for triumph of the morn
    Wherein the Child of bliss was born.

Let each religious soul then rise
To offer up a sacrifice,
And on the wings of pray'r and praise
His grateful heart to Heaven raise;
    For this, that in a stable lies,
      This poor neglected Babe, is he,
        Hell and Death that must control,
      And speak the blessed word, 'Be free,'

To ev'ry true believing soul:
Death has no sting, nor Hell no prize,
Through his merits great, whilst we
Travel to eternity,
And with the blessed angels sing
Hosannahs to the heav'nly King.

CHORUS

Rise, then, O rise! and let your voices
Tell the spheres the soul rejoices.
In Beth'lem, this auspicious morn,
The glorious Son of God is born.
The Child of glory, Prince of Peace,
Brings mercy that will never cease;
Merits that wipe away the sin
Each human soul was forfeit in;
And washing off the fatal stain,
Man to his Maker knits again:
Join then your grateful notes, and sing
Hosannahs to the heav'nly King.

Vera's First Christmas Adventure

ARNOLD BENNETT

Descriptions of life in the 'Five Towns' (that form present day Stoke-on-Trent) are the hallmark of one of Staffordshire's most famous writers. Bennett worked as a journalist before becoming a novelist who brought a depth of feeling and an observation for a certain detail of everyday things in his Potteries novels.

I

Five days before Christmas, Cheswardine came home to his wife from a week's sojourn in London on business. Vera, in her quality of the best-dressed woman in Bursley, met him on the doorstep (or thereabouts) of their charming but childless home, attired in a teagown that would have ravished a far less impressionable male than her husband; while he, in his quality of a prosaic and flourishing earthenware manufacturer, pretended to take the teagown as a matter of course, and gave her the sober, solid kiss of a man who has been married six years and is getting used to it.

Still, the teagown had pleased him, and by certain secret

symptoms Vera knew that it had pleased him. She hoped much from that teagown. She hoped that he had come home in a more pacific temper than he had shown when he left her, and that she would carry her point after all.

Now, naturally, when a husband in easy circumstances, the possessor of a pretty and pampered wife, spends a week in London and returns five days before Christmas, certain things are rightly and properly to be expected from him. It would need an astounding courage, an amazing lack of a sense of the amenity of conjugal existence in such a husband to enable him to disappoint such reasonable expectations. And Cheswardine, though capable of pulling the curb very tight on the caprices of his wife, was a highly decent fellow. He had no intention to disappoint; he knew his duty.

So that during afternoon tea with the teagown in a cosy corner of the great Chippendale drawing-room he began to unfasten a small wooden case which he had brought into the house in his own hand, opened it with considerable precaution, making a fine mess of packing-stuff on the carpet, and gradually drew to light a pair of vases of Venetian glass. He put them on the mantelpiece.

'There!' he said, proudly, and with a virtuous air.

They were obviously costly antique vases, exquisite in form, exquisite in the gradated tints of their pale blue and rose.

'Seventeenth century!' he said.

'They're very nice,' Vera agreed, with a show of enthusiasm. 'What are they for?'

'Your Christmas present,' Cheswardine explained, and added 'my dear!'

'Oh, Stephen!' she murmured.

A kiss on these occasions is only just, and Cheswardine had one.

'Duveens told me they were quite unique,' he said, modestly; 'and I believe 'em.'

A festive window display probably at Brookfield's shop, Stafford, about 1905

You might imagine that a pair of Venetian vases of the seventeenth century, stated by Duveens to be unique, would have satisfied a woman who had a generous dress allowance and lacked absolutely nothing that was essential. But Vera was not satisfied. She was, on the contrary, profoundly disappointed. For the presence of those vases proved that she had not carried her point. They deprived her of hope. The unpleasantness before Cheswardine went to London had been more or less *à propos* of a Christmas present. Vera had seen in Bostock's vast emporium in the neighbouring town of Hanbridge, a music-stool in the style known as *art nouveau*, which had enslaved her fancy. She had taken her husband to see it, and it had not enslaved her husband's fancy in the slightest degree. It was made in light woods, and the woods

were curved and twisted as though they had recently spent seven years in a purgatory for sinful trees. Here and there in the design onyx-stones had been set in the wood. The seat itself was beautifully soft. What captured Vera was chiefly the fact that it did not open at the top, as most elaborate music-stools do, but at either side. You pressed a button (onyx) and the panel fell down displaying your music in little compartments ready to hand; and the eastern moiety of the music-stool was for piano pieces, and the western moiety for songs. In short, it was the last word of music-stools; nothing could possibly be newer.

But Cheswardine did not like it, and did not conceal his opinion. He argued that it would not 'go' with the Chippendale furniture, and Vera said that all beautiful things 'went' together, and Cheswardine admitted that they did, rather dryly. You see, they took the matter seriously because the house was their hobby; they were always changing its interior, which was more than they could have done for a child, even if they had had one; and Cheswardine's finer and soberer taste was always fighting against Vera's predilection for the novel and the bizarre. Apart from clothes, Vera had not much more than the taste of a mouse.

They did not quarrel in Bostock's. Indeed, they did not quarrel anywhere; but after Vera had suggested that he might at any rate humour her by giving her the music-stool for a Christmas present (she seemed to think this would somehow help it to 'go' with the Chippendale), and Cheswardine had politely but firmly declined, there had been a certain coolness and quite six tears. Vera had caused it to be understood that even if Cheswardine was *not* interested in music, even if he did hate music and did call the Broadwood ebony grand ugly, that was no reason why she should be deprived of a pretty and original music-stool that would keep her music tidy and that

would be *hers*. As for it not going with the Chippendale, that was simply an excuse . . . etc.

Hence it is not surprising that the Venetian vases of the seventeenth century left Vera cold, and that the domestic prospects for Christmas were a little cold.

However, Vera, with wifely and submissive tact made the best of things; and that evening she began to decorate the hall, dining-room, and drawing-room with holly and mistletoe. Before the pair retired to rest, the true Christmas feeling, slightly tinged with a tender melancholy, permeated the house, and the servants were growing excited in advance. The servants weren't going to have a dinner-party, with crackers and port and a table-centre unmatched in the Five Towns; the servants weren't going to invite their friends to an evening's jollity. The servants were merely going to work somewhat harder and have somewhat less sleep; but such is the magical effect of holly and mistletoe twined round picture-cords and hung under chandeliers that the excitement of the servants was entirely pleasurable.

And as Vera shut the bedroom door, she said, with a delightful, forgiving smile –

'I saw a lovely cigar-cabinet at Bostock's yesterday.'

'Oh!' said Cheswardine, touched. He had no cigar-cabinet, and he wanted one, and Vera knew that he wanted one.

And Vera slept in the sweet consciousness of her thoughtful wifeliness.

The next morning, at breakfast, Cheswardine demanded –

'Getting pretty hard up, aren't you, Maria?'

He called her Maria when he wished to be arch.

'Well,' she said, 'as a matter of fact, I am. What with the _____'

And he gave her a five-pound note.

It happened so every year. He provided her with the money to buy him a Christmas present. But it is, I hope, unnecessary

to say that the connection between her present to him and the money he furnished was never crudely mentioned.

She made an opportunity, before he left for the works, to praise the Venetian vases, and she insisted that he should wrap up well, because he was showing signs of one of his bad colds.

II

In the early afternoon she went to Bostock's emporium, at Hanbridge, to buy the cigar-cabinet and a few domestic trifles. Bostock's is a good shop. I do not say that it has the classic and serene dignity of Brunt's, over the way, where one orders one's dining-room suites and one's frocks for the

Wintry Stoke-on-Trent scene about 1880

19

January dances. But it is a good shop, and one of the chief glories of the Paris of the Five Towns. It has frontages in three streets, and it might be called the shop of the hundred windows. You can buy pretty nearly anything at Bostock's, from an *art nouveau* music-stool up to the highest cheese – for there is a provision department. (You can't get cheese at Brunt's.)

Vera made her uninteresting purchases first, in the basement, and then she went up-stairs to the special Christmas department, which certainly was wonderful: a blaze and splendour of electric light; a glitter of gilded iridescent toys and knick-knacks; a smiling, excited, pushing multitude of faces, young and old; and the cashiers in their cages gathering in money as fast as they could lay their tired hands on it! A joyous, brilliant scene, calculated to bring soft tears of satisfaction to the board of directors that presided over Bostock's. It was a record Christmas for Bostock's. The electric cars were thundering over the frozen streets of all the Five Towns to bring customers to Bostock's. Children dreamt of Bostock's. Fathers went to scoff and remained to pay. Brunt's was not exactly alarmed, for nothing could alarm Brunt's; but there was just a sort of suspicion of something in the air at Brunt's that did not make for odious self-conceit. People seemed to become intoxicated when they went into Bostock's, to lose their heads in a frenzy of buying.

And there the *art nouveau* music-stool stood in the corner, where Vera had originally seen it! She approached it, not thinking of the terrible danger. The compartments for music lay invitingly open.

'Four pounds, nine and six, Mrs Cheswardine,' said a shopwalker, who knew her.

She stopped to finger it.

Well, of course everybody is acquainted with that peculiar ecstasy that undoubtedly does overtake you in good shops,

sometimes, especially at Christmas. I prefer to call it ecstasy rather than intoxication, but I have heard it called even drunkenness. It is a magnificent and overwhelming experience, like a good wine. A blind instict seizes your reason and throws her out of the window of your soul, and then assumes entire control of the volitional machinery. You listen to no arguments, you care for no consequences. You want a thing; you must have it; you do have it.

Vera was caught unawares by this magnificent and overwhelming experience, just as she stooped to finger the music-stool. A fig for the cigar-cabinet! A fig for her husband's objections! After all she was a grown-up woman (twenty-nine or thirty), and entitled to a certain freedom. She was not and would not be a slave. It would look perfect in the drawing-room.

'I'll take it,' she said.

'Yes, Mrs Cheswardine. A unique thing, quite unique. Penkethman!'

And Vera followed Penkethman to a cash desk and received half-a-guinea out of a five-pound note.

'I want it carefully packed,' said Vera.

'Yes, ma'am. It will be delivered in the morning.'

She was just beginning to realize that she had been under the sinister influence of the ecstasy, and that she had not bought the cigar-cabinet, and that she had practically no more money, and that Stephen's rule against credit was the strictest of all his rules, when she caught sight of Mr Charles Woodruff buying toys, doubtless for his nephews and nieces.

Mr Woodruff was the bachelor friend of the family. He had loved Vera before Stephen loved her, and he was still attached to her. Stephen and he were chums of the most advanced kind. Why! Stephen and Vera thought nothing of bickering in front of Mr Woodruff, who rated them both and sided with neither.

'Hello!' said Woodruff, flushing, and moving his long,

clumsy limbs when she touched him on the shoulder. 'I'm just buying a few toys.'

She helped him to buy toys, and then he asked her to go and have tea with him at the newly-opened Sub Rosa Tea Rooms, in Machin Street. She agreed, and, in passing the music-stool, gave a small parcel which she was carrying to Penkethman, and told him he might as well put it in the music-stool. She was glad to have tea with Charlie Woodruff. It would distract her, prevent her from thinking. The ecstasy had almost died out, and she had a violent desire not to think.

III

A terrible blow fell upon her the next morning. Stephen had one of his bad colds, one of his worst. The mere cold she could have supported with fortitude, but he was forced to remain indoors, and his presence in the house she could not support with fortitude. The music-stool would be sure to arrive before lunch, and he would be there to see it arrive. The ecstasy had fully expired now, and she had more leisure to think than she wanted. She could not imagine what mad instinct had compelled her to buy the music-stool. (Once out of the shop these instincts aways are difficult to imagine.) She knew that Stephen would be angry. He might perhaps go to the length of returning the music-stool whence it came. For, though she was a pretty and pampered woman, Stephen had a way, in the last resort, of being master in his own house. And she could not even placate him with the gift of a cigar-cabinet. She could not buy a five-guinea cigar-cabinet with ten and six. She had no other money in the world. She never had money, yet money was always running through her fingers. Stephen treated her generously, gave her an ample allowance, but he would under no circumstances permit credit, nor would he pay her allowance in advance. She had nothing to expect till the New Year.

She attended to his cold, and telephoned to the works for a clerk to come up, and she refrained from telling Stephen that he must have been very careless while in London, to catch a cold like that. Her self-denial in this respect surprised Stephen, but he put it down to the beneficent influence of Christmas and the Venetian vases.

Bostock's pair-horse van arrived before the garden gate earlier than her worst fears had anticipated, and Bostock's men were evidently in a tremendous hurry that morning. In quite an abnormally small number of seconds the wooden case containing the fragile music-stool was lying in the inner hall, waiting to be unpacked. Having signed the delivery-book Vera stood staring at the accusatory package. Stephen was lounging over the dining-room fire, perhaps dozing. She would have the thing swiftly transported up-stairs and hidden in an attic for a time.

But just then Stephen popped out of the dining-room. Stephen's masculine curiosity had been aroused by the advent of Bostock's van. He had observed the incoming of the package from the window, and he had ventured to the hall to inspect it. The event had roused him wonderfully from the heavy torpor which a cold induces. He wore a dressing-gown, the pockets of which bulged with handkerchiefs.

'You oughtn't to be out here, Stephen,' said his wife.

'Nonsense!' he said. 'Why, upon my soul, this steam heat is warmer than the dining-room fire.'

Vera, silenced by the voice of truth, could not reply.

Stephen bent his great height to inspect the package. It was an appetizing Christmas package; straw escaped from between its ribs, and it had an air of being filled with something at once large and delicate.

'Oh!' observed Stephen, humorously. 'Ah! So this is it, is it? Ah! Oh! Very good!'

And he walked round it.

How on earth had he learnt that she had bought it? She had not mentioned the purchase to Mr Woodruff.

'Yes, Stephen,' she said timidly. 'That's it, and I hope——'

'It ought to hold a tidy few cigars, that ought,' remarked Stephen complacently.

He took it for the cigar-cabinet!

She paused, struck. She had to make up her mind in an instant.

'Oh yes,' she murmured.

'A thousand?'

'Yes, a thousand,' she said.

'I thought so,' murmured Stephen. 'I mustn't kiss you, because I've got a cold,' said he. 'But, all the same I'm awfully obliged, Vera. Suppose we have it opened now, eh? Then we could decide where it is to go, and I could put my cigars in it.'

'Oh no,' she protested. 'Oh no, Stephen! That's not fair! It mustn't be opened before Christmas morning.'

'But I gave you my vases yesterday.'

'That's different,' she said. 'Christmas is Christmas.'

'Oh, very well,' he yielded. 'That's all right, my dear.'

Then he began to sniff.

'There's a deuced odd smell from it,' he said.

'Perhaps it's the wood!' she faltered.

'I hope it isn't,' he said. 'I expect it's the straw. A deuced odd smell. We'll have the thing put in the side hall, next to the clock. It will be out of the way there. And I can come and gaze at it when I feel depressed. Eh, Maria?' He was undoubtedly charmed at the prospect of owning so large and precious a cigar-cabinet.

Considering that the parcel which she had given to Penkethman to put in the music-stool comprised half-a-pound of Bostock's very ripest Gorgonzola cheese, bought at the cook's special request, the smell which proceeded from the

mysterious inwards of the packing-case did not surprise Vera at all. But it disconcerted her none the less. And she wondered how she could get the cheese out.

For thirty hours the smell from the unopened packing-case waxed in vigour and strength. Stephen's cold grew worse and prevented him from appreciating its full beauty, but he savoured enough of it to induce him to compare it facetiously to the effluvium of a dead rat, and he said several times that Bostock's really ought to use better straw. He was frequently to be seen in the hall, gloating over his cigar-cabinet. Once he urged Vera to have it opened and so get rid of the straw, but she refused, and found the nerve to tell him that he was exaggerating the odour.

She was at a loss what to do. She could not get up in the middle of the night and unpack the package and hide its guilty secret. Indeed, to unpack the package would bring about her ruin instantly; for, the package unpacked, Stephen would naturally expect to see the cigar-cabinet. And so the hours crept on to Christmas and Vera's undoing. She gave herself a headache.

It was just thirty hours after the arrival of the package when Mr Woodruff dropped in for tea. Stephen was asleep in the dining-room, which apartment he particularly affected during his colds. Woodruff was shown into the drawing-room, where Vera was having her headache. Vera brightened. In fact, she suddenly grew very bright. And she gave Woodruff tea, and took some herself, and Woodruff passed an enjoyable twenty minutes.

The two Venetian vases were on the mantelpiece. Vera rose into ecstasies about them, and called upon Charlie Woodruff to rise too. He got up from his chair to examine the vases, which Vera had placed close together side by side at the corner of the mantelpiece nearest to him. Vera and Woodruff also stood close together side by side. And just as Woodruff

was about to handle the vases, Vera knocked his arm; his arm collided with one vase; that vase collided with the next, and both fell to earth – to the hard, unfeeling, unyielding tiles of the hearth.

IV

They were smashed to atoms.
Vera screamed. She screamed twice, and ran out of the room.

'Stephen, Stephen!' she cried hysterically. 'Charlie has broken my vases, both of them. It *is* too bad of him. He's really too clumsy!'

There was a terrific pother. Stephen wakened violently, and in a moment all three were staring ineffectually at the thousand crystal fragments on the hearth.

'But——' began Charlie Woodruff.

And that was all he did say.

He and Vera and Stephen had been friends since infancy, so she had the right not to conceal her feelings before him; Stephen had the same right. They both exercised it.

'But——' began Charlie again.

'Oh, never mind,' Stephen stopped him curtly. 'Accidents can't be helped.'

'I shall get another pair,' said Woodruff.

'No, you won't,' replied Stephen. 'You can't. There isn't another pair in the world. See?'

The two men simultaneously perceived that Vera was weeping. She was very pretty in tears, but that did not prevent the masculine world from feeling awkward and self-conscious. Charlie had notions about going out and burying himself.

'Come, Vera, come,' her husband enjoined, blowing his nose with unnecessary energy, bad as his cold was.

'I – I liked those vases more than anything you've –

26

you've ever given me,' Vera blubbered, charmingly, patting her eyes.

Stephen glanced at Woodruff, as who should say: 'Well, my boy, you uncorked those tears, I'll leave you to deal with 'em. You see, I'm an invalid in a dressing-gown. I leave you.'

And went.

'No-but-look-here-I-say,' Charlie Woodruff expostulated to Vera when he was alone with her – he often started an expostulation with that singular phrase. 'I'm awfully sorry. I don't know how it happened. You must let me give you something else.'

Vera shook her head.

'No,' she said. 'I wanted Stephen awfully to give me that music-stool that I told you about a fortnight ago. But he gave me the vases instead, and I liked them ever so much better.'

'I shall give you the music-stool. If you wanted it a fortnight ago, you want it now. It won't make up for the vases, of course, but——'

'No, no,' said Vera, positively.

'Why not?'

'I do not wish you to give me anything. It wouldn't be quite nice,' Vera insisted.

'But I give you something every Christmas.'

'Do you?' asked Vera, innocently.

'Yes, and you and Stephen give me something.'

'Besides, Stephen doesn't quite like the music-stool.'

'What's that got to do with it? You like it. I'm giving it to you, not to him. I shall go over to Bostock's to-morrow morning and get it.'

'I forbid you to.'

'I shall.'

Woodruff departed.

Within five minutes the Cheswardine coachman was driving off in the dogcart to Hanbridge, with the packing-case in the

back of the cart, and a note. He brought back the cigar-cabinet. Stephen had not stirred from the dining-room, afraid to encounter a tearful wife. Presently his wife came into the dining-room bearing the vast load of the cigar-cabinet in her delicate arms.

'I thought it might amuse you to fill it with your cigars – just to pass the time,' she said.

Stephen's thought was: 'Well, women take the cake.' It was a thought that occurs frequently to the husbands of Veras.

There was ripe Gorgonzola at dinner. Stephen met it as one meets a person whom one fancies one has met somewhere but cannot remember where.

The next afternoon the music-stool came, for the second time, into the house. Charlie brought it in *his* dogcart. It was unpacked ostentatiously by the radiant Vera. What could Stephen say in depreciation of the gift from their oldest and best friend? As a fact he could and did say a great deal. But he said it when he happened to be all alone in the drawing-room, and had observed the appalling way in which that music-stool did not 'go' with the Chippendale.

'Look at the d—— thing!' he exclaimed to himself. 'Look at it!'

However, the Christmas dinner-party was a brilliant success, and after it Vera sat on the *art nouveau* music-stool and twittered songs, and what with her being so attractive and birdlike, and what with the Christmas feeling in the air . . . well, Stephen resigned himself to the music-stool.

from

Daisy's Lichfield

DAISY WINDER

'Why don't you write it all down?' said a friend to Daisy Winder when she described the street in which she lived as a child. Lichfield's Stowe Street is recalled in the memories of a twenties childhood.

Then came Christmas; to our family a bit of a mixed blessing. I always loved Christmas, and still do, but for us the last week before it was a bit of a nightmare because many of the gentry, (oh yes, we had some), would bring their poultry to Mam to be dressed – ducks, geese and chickens to be ready by Christmas Eve. This is where our big tin bath came in useful. We would all sit round it plucking the feathers off. We children did the soft feathers – breast, backs and legs – and Mam would do wings and tails, because our little fingers were not strong enough.

I learned to pluck and dress chickens at an early age, didn't mind those, but geese were terrible to do, especially if the owners wanted the feathers back and you had to keep them separate. The house smelt of burning feathers and singeing birds all over Christmas. Our labours bore fruit though, because Mam was able to buy extras for us all. I know that every Christmas morning we would have a large pork pie for breakfast, the best I ever tasted, and we would have fruit and

Christmas lights in Market Street, Lichfield

real cream for tea, and all of us had a nice present – we were lucky.

People helped us out. There was one lady who owned the Seven Stars pub, Dad's local, and every year just before Christmas my Dad would kill and dress one of her pigs, (what a versatile lot we were). She didn't pay him cash, but would supply him with beer over a period of time. She gave us all the goodies from the pig, like lard and all the innards. We made pig's pudding, scratchings, chitterlings and faggots. These were riches to us; we got the benefit.

I think that Dad was a bit afraid of her. She used to throw him out when she thought that he'd had enough to drink. She was a very large lady, with bright red hair, nobody argued with her. She would say to Dad, 'Now then, Bill, you get off home to your wife and kids', and he would come home like a

lamb. Once he won the football sweep – about three pounds, a large sum in those days, but she wouldn't give Dad all the money. She brought half to Mam, and Dad didn't dare say a word. She helped a lot of her customers' families; it was a sad day when she gave up.

Lines on the Approach of Winter

THOMAS BAKEWELL

Dubbed the 'Moorland Poet', Thomas Bakewell also had an interest in the provision for the mentally ill and operated by all accounts a successful private asylum. A native of Cheadle, he belonged to the 'St Thomas's Club', a social club which restricted membership to persons whose Christian name was Thomas.

When trees their leaves begin to shed,
And rustling in my path are spread,
I sigh when first the sound I hear,
For winter then is drawing near.

When swallows in great numbers meet,
And twitt'ring do each other greet;

Definitive proof that 'winter' is now near at New Buildings Farm,
King's Bromley

Their quick departure then I fear,
And think that winter now is near.

When red-breasts* do most sweetly sing,
And rival e'en the birds of spring,
Tho' I do love their notes to hear,
They prove that winter now is near.

In various tints the groves are seen,
From brown to deepest shades of green:
Tho' sights like these the eye may cheer,
They prove that winter now is near.

* The young birds of this kind will begin to sing in August, and keep
improving till severe weather puts a stop to their sweet notes.

And when the huntsman's mellow horn,
Cheerly awakes the slumb'ring morn;
These sounds, tho' pleasing to the ear,
Do also prove that winter's near.

When spaniels snuff the tainted gale,
And the quick gunner, stout and hale,
Marks the flush'd covey, wing'd with fear,
It proves that winter now is near.

When first I hear the curfew bell,
Solemn the hour of evening tell,
I sadden at the sound so drear,
And think that winter now is near.

When low'ring storms, with gloomy sweep,
Do o'er yon misty mountains creep,
And gazing herds stand chill'd with fear,
It proves that winter now is near.

Then turn to those blest shores above,
From whence the joys shall ne'er remove,
Nor feel sad changes of the year;
For one eternal spring reigns there.

Christmas Definitions

SAMUEL JOHNSON

Lichfield's literary giant began planning in 1747 to publish his great Dictionary of the English Language *which formed the basis of modern lexicography. It was published in 1755.*

CHRI'STMAS. *n.ſ* [from *Chriſt* and *maſs.*] The day on which the nativity of our blessed Saviour is celebrated, by the particular ſervice of the church.

A CHRISTMAS-BOX. *n.ſ.* [from *chriſtmas* and *box.*] A box in which little presents are collected at Christmas.
When time comes round, a *Chriſtmas-box* they bear,
And one day makes them rich for all the year.   *Gay's Trivia*

CHRISTMAS-FLOWER. *n.ſ.* See HELLEBORE.

HE'LLEBORE *n.ſ.* [*helleborus*, Latin.] Chriſtmas flower.
It hath a digitated leaf: the flower conſiſts of ſeveral leaves placed orbicularly, and expanding in form of a roſe: in the centre of the flower riſes the pointal, encompaſſed about the baſe with ſeveral little horns between the chives and petals, which turn to a fruit, in which the membranaceous huſks

are gathered into a little head, ending in an horn, opening
longwiſe, and full of roundiſh or oval ſeeds. *Miller.*

SNOW. *n.ſ.* [ſnaþ, Saxon; ſnee, Dutch.] The ſmall particles of
water frozen before they unite into drops. *Locke.*
Benaiah slew a lion in a pit, in time of *snow.* 2 *Sa.* xxiii.
Drought and heat conſume ſnow waters. *Job* xxiv. 19.
He gives the Winter's ſnow her airy birth,
And bids her virgin fleeces clothe the earth. *Sandys.*

TO SNOW. *v.n.* [ſnaþan, Saxon; ſneeuwen, Dutch.] To have ſnow fall.

TO SNOW. *v.a.* To ſcatter like ſnow.
If thou be'ſt born to ſee ſtrange ſights,
Ride ten thouſand days and nights,
'Till age ſnow white hairs on thee. *Donne.*

SNO'WBALL. *n.ſ.* [ſnow and *ball.*] A round lump of congelated
ſnow.
They paſſed to the eaſt-riding of Yorkſhire, their company
daily increaſing, like a ſnowball in rolling. *Hayward.*
His bulky folly gathers as it goes,
And, rolling o'er you, like a ſnowball grows. *Dryden.*
A ſnowball having the power to produce in us the ideas of
white, cold, and round, the powers, as they are in the
ſnowball, I call qualities; and as they are ſenſations in our
underſtandings, ideas. *Locke.*

SNOW-WHITE. *adj.* [ſnow and *white.*] White as ſnow.
A ſnow-white bull ſhall on your ſhore be ſlain;
His offer'd entrails caſt into the main. *Dryden's Æn.*

SNO'WY. *adj.* [from ſnow.]
1. White like ſnow.

Lichfield girl with Johnson's 'round lump of congelated snow'

So ſhews a ſnowy dove trooping with crows,
As yonder lady o'er her fellows ſhews.   *Shakeſpeare.*
Now I fee thy jolly train:
Snowy headed Winter leads,
Spring and summer next ſucceeds;
Yellow Autumn brings the rear;
Thou art father of the year.   *Rowe.*
The bluſhing ruby on her ſnowy breaſt,
Render'd its panting whiteneſs more confeſt.   *Prior.*
2. Abounding with ſnow.
Theſe firſt in Crete
And Ida known; thence on the ſnowy top
Of cold Olympus rul'd the middle air.   *Milton's Par. Loſt.*
As when the Tartar from his Ruſſian foe,
By Aſtracan, over the ſnowy plains,
Retires.   *Milton's Paradiſe Loſt.*

Winter Wonderland

PHIL DRABBLE

Television viewers have been delighted by Phil Drabble's
running commentaries of sheepdog trials and presentations of
other natural history programmes. Readers have been equally
pleased by his many newspaper articles and books which describe
the work on his own nature reserve on land surrounding his
Staffordshire home.

There is no silence, in a wood, like the silence when dry and powdery snow lies on the ground. It muffles every footfall so that grown and clumsy men drift through the trees as stealthily as their shadows. Birds, which have nothing to sing about in such weather, sit with feathers fluffed out to conserve their body heat more efficiently than an eiderdown.

The clatter as a wood pigeon flies up when he sees what he probably mistakes for a human ghost is as loud in contrast as a lorry disgorging a ton of bricks. Last weekend was different. The snow had come all right, but it was not dry and powdery. a gooey blanket, about a foot thick, was so wet that it congealed beneath every footfall into ice.

I often think how lucky I am to have chosen a job where I work from home with no boss but myself. I have been so busy this autumn that the current book I am writing has got shoved aside to make way for more urgent work until it is several weeks behind schedule.

Before I can get down to serious writing, the animals have to be watered and fed. Whatever the weather. This is not much of a problem when the snow is dry and powdery, because it is only the work of a moment to scoop it aside and provide a dry bed to scatter the corn.

When I went out last Sunday morning, I could not open a single gate out of the yard. When I forced them a foot or so ajar, the snow behind congealed into hard ice and jammed the whole thing solid. I had to climb through the sitting-room window, which took me to the other side of the yard gates, and take a shovel to clear the snow behind the gates before I could start to feed at all.

Walking up the wood with a bucket of corn to feed the pheasants got me glowing with exhilaration and I stopped to admire the trees which had been coated with virgin snow. There was nothing silent about the wood now, though. Every few minutes there was a crack as sharp as a whiplash.

Pye Green, Cannock Chase, 1975

I thought at first it was an intruder with a rifle and was surprised that Belle, the Alsatian, took no notice. She never misses an invitation to see off uninvited guests which she regards as her brand of quarry.

She was wiser than I was, for the sound was not man-made. Every shattering crack was a branch weighed down by its burden of wet snow. It sorted out the weak and rotten first, leaving them to lie unlamented on the woodland floor where insects would invade them and birds would eat the insects.

But it was not only the rotten trees that suffered. The whole crown came out of an oak tree, fifty or sixty feet high. When I went to examine it to see if it was rotten in the heart, it was as sound as a bell. The weight of snow and the driving wind had shattered it into splinters as jagged as if it had been hit by lightning.

Hawthorn trees seemed to be the worst sufferers and one about twenty feet high and six inches across had fallen across the drive and brought down my neighbour's telephone wire. So the first job was to saw that up into pieces small enough for me to lug away before someone piled into my boundary fence trying to avoid it.

By that time, I was warmer than plenty of clerks sitting in centrally heated offices so I got out the old tractor to do a bit of snow clearing. I have made a Heath Robinson arrangement of an oak plank bolted to the back of the tractor so that it can be raised and lowered hydraulically. By dropping it on the ground and skating off in reverse at high speed, a huge wedge of snow is pushed backwards clearing the yard and entrance to the drive in about a quarter of an hour. It is a fiendishly cold job, done in cold blood, but an exhilarating experience after enough hard work to get the steam up.

Not all wildlife suffers as badly as you might think. Mice and voles are all right because they tunnel under the snow where their normal food is buried and, since they are out of

sight of hawks and owls, their chances of survival dwindle very little. Badgers grow lethargic and lie in their snug setts shamelessly and foxes get a few easy meals by catching almost anything which the cold overcomes.

But I watched a party of fallow deer actually cashing in on their misfortune. The grass was so deeply covered that they had to scratch through the snow to win every mouthful. But deer are tremendous browsers on trees. Although few leaves are showing, except honeysuckle, the sap is beginning to flow and buds are forming beneath the unappetising bark. They had already eaten what they could reach, but the weight of wet snow humbled many whippy saplings and made them bow towards the ground. The deer were wandering through the wood, nipping off the tasty buds as if some unseen hand were proffering them.

By the time I had done my chores, wandered through the wood and had my lunch, it was almost time to start to feed again. So the book is yet another day behind schedule.

Trench Warfare, Christmas 1914

From the outbreak through to the end of the First World War the North Staffordshire Regiment saw service on the Western Front. In the first phase of the war up to January 1915 battalion casualties were horrific with a loss of 489 lives. There is the often told almost mythical tale of a Christmas truce football match, but here from the History of The 1st & 2nd Battalions The North Staffordshire Regiment (The Prince of Wales') 1914–1923 *comes the reality of a temporary cessation in hostilities.*

On November 19th the North Staffords went into billets at the Lunatic Asylum at ARMENTIERES, where the men got baths and an opportunity to clean up generally. Each night two Companies went to the line to work on communication trenches.

The period of Trench Warfare had now definitely commenced, with its alternate tours of trenches and billets, combined with plenty of hard work at all times.

The Battalion took over trenches from the 2nd Leinsters on November 23rd and was in turn relieved by them on November 29th. Apart from the terribly wet and muddy state of the trenches there was nothing of interest to record. All available men were employed making a causeway from Battalion Headquarters to the front line, as communication trenches were impassable, owing to the depth of water everywhere.

On December 2nd H.M. the King and H.R.H. the Prince of Wales visited the 6th Division and shook hands with all Commanding Officers and Adjutants. On December 11th the 1st North Staffords took over trenches in the RUE DU BOIS area, generally known as the 'Death Trap' or 'Dead Man's Alley,' and remained there till relieved on December 31st. The trenches were in an even worse condition than during the last tour. They were well over knee deep in mud and water, and all reliefs had to take place over the open.

The 24th and 25th December, 1914, saw the extraordinary spectacle of an unofficial truce between our troops and the

Sapper Thomas Brough from Cannock was sadly the 1915 Christmas Day victim of the sniper

Saxons who were opposite. On Christmas Eve 'C' Company was holding the left section of the Battalion front, with 'A' Company on its right. Everything had been normal up to evening 'Stand down' and the Company Commander was having his supper in the Headquarters dug-out, when the Company Sergeant-Major put his head in and said 'What am I to do, Sir? The Germans are sitting on their parapets, lighting candles and singing hymns!' The Company Commander at once went out and mounting on the fire step saw small lights all along the German trenches and heard many voices uplifted in song.

He decided to consult with the Officer Commanding 'A' Company, who was the Senior Officer in the front line, and accordingly started to make his way down the trench towards 'A' Company Headquarters. On his way he surprised one of his men in the act of climbing out of the trench and discovered that there was a German soldier in 'No man's land,' who wanted to speak to a British soldier, so ordering his own man back, he slipped out himself to investigate.

The German turned out to be a private soldier who had been a waiter at Brighton, and was anxious to exchange cigars for bully beef. The Company Commander asked to be taken to an Officer, and was conducted to the German front line, where he found a group of German Officers standing by the wall of a ruined farm house. They were very suspicious and asked repeatedly if he was armed. 'Word of a Gentleman.' He was not and said so, and finally his word was accepted. Christmas greetings were interchanged and finally the suggestion was made that Christmas Day might be observed as a day of rest and that the Infantry should not fire on each other, though of course, neither side could answer for their Artillery.

It was then agreed that all Infantry fire should cease

forthwith and that the informal truce should continue until 11 p.m. (12 midnight German time) on Christmas night.

The German spokesman now asked for permission to bury the dead with whose frozen corpses 'No man's land' was strewn. The Company Commander, who was a very junior Officer, felt that he was getting rather out of his depth, and replied that a senior Officer would have to deal with that question. He accordingly went back to his own front line, and seeking out the Officer commanding 'A' Company, explained the situation to him. The latter had no qualms, and immediately went out and arranged for burial parties from both sides to leave their trenches at 10 a.m. on Christmas Day, each side to bury the dead in their own half of 'No man's land.'

The remainder of the night passed in absolute peace, and at 10 a.m. on Christmas Day, parties of men armed only with picks and shovels, sallied forth from either side. Ten minutes later the inevitable corpse was found astride the half-way line and in no time the burial parties were merged in fraternal disorder.

Some Uhlan Officers, who had been transferred to the Infantry, came out and posed for their photographs in the centre of a group of British and German soldiery. They were magnificently polished and clean, which unfortunately, the British Officers were not.

During all this time sufficient men were kept posted in our trenches to check any attempt at treachery and to prevent any of the enemy entering our trenches. The Germans evidently took the same precautions, for when Captain Ewald tried to get a peep into their front trench, he was promptly warned off by an invisible sentry.

As soon as the truce started the Saxons advised our men to warn the Battalions on their right to stop in their trenches as they were opposed by Prussians, described as 'Bosen Kerle' (surly ruffians).

At dusk the men of both sides returned to their trenches, but no hostile act followed the expiry of the truce at 11 p.m.

Shortly after 'Stand down' next morning 'C' Company Commander was informed that a German Officer wished to speak to him in 'No man's land.' On going out he found a very polite and spotless individual awaiting him, who, after an exchange of compliments, informed him that his Colonel had given orders for a renewal of hostilities at mid-day and might the men be warned to keep down, please? 'C' Company Commander thanked the German Officer for his courtesy, whereupon, saluting and bowing from the waist, he replied, 'We are Saxons; you are Anglo Saxons; word of a gentleman is for us as for you.'

The troops were duly warned to keep down, but just before hostilities were due to re-open a tin was thrown into 'A' Company's lines with a piece of paper in it bearing the inscription,

Burslem's published postcard of First World War Cannock Chase army camp

46

'We shoot to the air' and sure enough, at the appointed hour a few vague shots wre fired high over the trenches. Then all was quiet again and the unofficial truce continued.

There are many stories current as to how the Christmas, 1914, unofficial truce started, but the above is vouched for by one of the Officers present throughout.

The Battalion was relieved on the night of December 31st, and went into billets at CHAPELLE D'ARMENTIERES.

The month of January, 1915, was uneventful, being spent alternately in the trenches and in billets at the Lunatic Asylum.

For the first three weeks the weather was very bad, with almost continuous rain, and conditions in the trenches became appalling. There was water everywhere and in places it was four feet deep. An attempt was made to prevent the water rising by means of hand pumps, which were kept going day and night, but these had little effect owing to there being no fall in the ground in any direction. The only consolation was that the enemy's trenches were evidently in a similar condition, as shells falling into them threw up columns of water everywhere.

The First Christmas Eve

ROBERT WILLIAMS BUCHANAN

*Born at Caverswall Robert Williams Buchanan established his
reputation with poetry that displayed a strong lyrical and
narrative streak reminiscent of his Scottish background. This
extract, which is only part of a longer section, comes from* The
Outcast: a rhyme for the time *which was published in
1891. His style is in sharp contrast to the Pre-Raphaelites
whom he attacked for their sensuality.*

'A WORLD without a God! Heigho! . . .
The good old God had merit, though!
Le Bon Dieu, gravely interfering
   In all Humanity's affairs,
Bowing His kind gray head and hearing
   The orphan's moans, the widow's prayers,
Was worth, or so it seems to me,
Whole cataracts of Tendency;
For though He now and then grew crusty,
And damn'd some few (as all gods must), He
Was patient 'spite deep provocation
With the small things of His creation!
Jesus He loved, and tolerated
   Even Goethe's patronising nod!

Helping to dig the neighbours out in Hednesford Street, Cannock

Century on century He waited
While great philosophers debated,
　　Then, finding men dispense with 'God,'
Took His departure from the earth,
　　Where still some limbs were genuflected,
The day that Schopenhauer had birth, –
　　And left the human race dejected!'

Without, while in my chambers dreary
　　I mused and watch'd the flickering flame,
The snow fell thickly, night winds weary
Moaned *miserere! miserere!*
　　And shivering revellers went and came.
Twas Christmas Eve! The bells were ringing
　　In faintly joyful jubilation:

49

A Staffordshire Christmas

I heard the tidings they were bringing
   But groan'd apart in indignation.
My plans in life had all miscarried;
My only friends were dead, or married;
My book (that Epic you remember)
   Had gone to wrap up cheese and butter;
And lonely, in the lone December,
   As feebly as a leaf may flutter
From bough to bough while bleak winds blow,
   Till rough feet tread it in the mire,
This heart of mine had sunken low,
   Dead to the world and its desire!
'Confound their superstitious revels!'
   I murmur'd, spirit-sick and sour,
'I'll dine with Care and the blue devils
   And curse the world with Schopenhauer!
There is no God, and all men know it
Except the preacher and the poet;
Women are slaves and men are flunkeys,
The best but well-developed monkeys,
And Virtue is – a huswive's sampler,
   Self-sacrifice – an usurer's chatter;
Once Heaven was sure and Hope was ampler,
   But now the Devil rules Mind and Matter!
Le Roi est mort – destroy'd and undone,
   Or impotent and deaf and blind –
So *vive le Roi* of Hell and London,
   Who weaves a shroud for Humankind!'

Peace upon earth! goodwill to men!
   The bells rang out with sad vibrations.
I poked the fire, pursued again
   My misanthropic meditations.

'The last new Philosophic Pill,
A panacea for every ill,
Is – 'Quit thy service in the Shrine
Prophets and seers have deemed divine,
Give up the Sphynx's dark acrostic,
Be neither atheist nor agnostic,
But, since thy days are just a span,
Worship and praise the new God, MAN!
He shall endure when thou art dust,
    Gain that of which thou art bereaven,
He shall absorb thy love and trust,
Thy dying struggles shall adjust
    The ladder which He climbs to heaven!
The better thou, the grander He,
This god of thee and thine, shall be!
And in the thought of His perfection,
    To which all creatures are proceeding,
Thy soul shall 'scape from its dejection
    Caused by too much eclectic reading!'
Service of Man, – or Monkey! Far
Better to sit rectangular,
And like a dervish contemplate
    My very navel till it grows
The central whirligig of Fate,
    The Rose of Heaven that burns and blows!
Better to dance with barefoot souls,
Like good John Calvin, on hot coals,
And, full of sin yet grace-deserving,
Face the Arch-enemy without swerving!
But worship MAN? Go back once more
To image-worship as of yore,
And bend my head and bow my knee
To this King Ape, Humanity?
This stomach-troubled, squirming, aching,

Mud-wallowing, creature of a day,
This criticising, this book-making,
Fretful, dyspeptic, thing of clay!
This Multi-face whom it hath taken
Ages to learn to wash and dress!
This horde of swine, doom'd to be bacon,
And now, by countless devils o'ertaken,
Shrieking in impotent distress!
This mass of foulness and of folly
Through whom the Paracletes have died!
This Yuletide carcase deck'd with holly
In honour of its Crucified!
Now great Jehovah lies o'erthrown,
Shall the mere Pigmy reign at last?
Pshaw, rather worship stick or stone,
And let Humanity crawl past!

'Man as an individual, I
Hold first of creatures 'neath the sky,
But though I'm human at the best,
Man the Abstraction I detest!
Collectively, this Human Race,
Despite its brag and self-acclaim,
Its pride, its pompous talk, is base;
Ever, in every clime and place,
Its record is of sin and shame!
Bright holocausts of martyr'd blood
Mark its progression up the ages;
The sensual protoplasmic mud
Bespatters even its Seers and Sages!
Nay, what are all the human crew
But maggots from corruption bred? –
"By heaven, we talk like gods, and do
Like dogs!" Nat Field has wisely said!

'True spirit of Christmas' during a 1979 procession at Lichfield Cathedral

'A poor half-witted Caliban,
    Wailing his nature and condition,
Still prone upon the mud, is Man,
    And ne'er can be his own Magician.
Far less, far less, his own supreme
    Master and Lord and Arbitrator!
Nay! till the stars shall cease to gleam,
The wretch shall blunder in a dream
    And say his *Noster in cœlum Pater!*
In Heaven (or if you please, in Hell)
    Must reign the Lord of man and woman –
Not 'mid these shadows where we dwell,
Not on this blood-stain'd sward where fell
    The foolish gods who have loved the Human.

Nay, man can ne'er by man be shriven,
    By borrow'd rays his star must shine,
Not threefold heritage in Heaven
Could purge his spirit of its leaven,
    Or make the Upright Beast divine!'

. . . While thus I mused, I heard without
    A foot that blunder'd on the stair,
Then sounds of one who groped about
To find a door – 'Some dun, no doubt!'
    I thought, not rising from my chair.
Then some one softly knock'd. I stirred not,
But sat stone-still as if I heard not. . . .
Again! – 'Come in,' at last I cried,
Whereon the door flew open wide,
And on the threshold there was seen
A Stranger, elegant of mien,
Tall, white-shirt-fronted and dress-suited,
Faultlessly gloved and neatly booted,
Who, paletot upon his arm,
    Opera hat upon his head,
Smiled at my start of vague alarm,
    And pausing ere he enter'd, said –
'Pardon this call so unexpected.
    I sail from England, sir, to-morrow,
And to your room have been directed
    A little kind advice to borrow.
If I have been instructed rightly
    You are a Poet, and the man
I seek for' (here he bow'd politely), –
    'I'm sure you'll help me if you can.'
So saying, he closed the door behind him,
    And threw his coat upon a chair,
While I, a little piqued to find him

So confident and debonair,
Cried, 'Who the Devil are *you?*'
                               The light
Fell on his features waxen white,
His raven ringlets thinly threaded
With silver as he stood bareheaded,
His black moustache, and underneath
Two pearl-white rows of smiling teeth.
'The Devil?' he cried. 'Pray, did you mention
That very primitive invention,
Who surely, whatsoe'er cognomen
    You give him – Satan, Ahrimanes,
Baal, Moloch – though he awes old women,
    The merest fiction of the brain is?
The Poets have invented for us
Some six or seven Fiends that bore us –
Chiefly the one your gentle Milton
Set the high buskin and the stilt on,
And taught to make speech after speech to
A God extremely given to preach, too!
Nay, Goethe even, though well acquainted
With his infernal subject, painted
A fiend impossibly malicious
And supernaturally vicious.
Sir, the real Devil, Science teaches,
Not only wears man's hat and breeches,
But shares Humanity's affliction.
In short, sir, Satan is a fiction,
Save in so far as we sad creatures
Assume his airs and ape his features

I listened in amaze, while he,
Smiling at my perplexity,
Advance into the room and stood

Full in the firelight's crimson glow, –
A lithe, tall form of flesh and blood,
   Yet pallid as the bloodless snow:
A modern shape such as we meet
   Cigar in mouth and homeward strolling
After the play, in Regent Street,
Where Phryne trips with loitering feet
   And lissome Lais goes patrolling.

Answering his smile I cried, 'Who is it?
Your name? and why this midnight visit?
Fixing on me his bright black eyes,
'A poet, sir, should recognise,'
He answer'd, 'one who has so long,
Been theme for satire and for song!
I' faith, I am somewhat widely famed
As PHILIP VANDERDECKEN, *named*
The FLYING DUTCHMAN!'

                    As he spake
I seemed to hear the surges break
On some steep shores, while thunder-crashes
Answer'd the Tempest's fiery flashes!
My head swam round – I shrank in dread
   From that world-famous Form of fiction.
'Pray calm yourself,' he laughing said,
   'For we are fellows in affliction!
The cliques have damn'd *you* too, I hear,
For many a melancholy year,
Because, in trying hard to double,
Against a stream of tears and trouble,
The Cape of Desolate Endeavour,
And reach Fame's Ocean (smooth for ever!)
You used bad language, loudly swearing,
For great or small gods little caring,

You'd toss on Life's mad Sea until
You'd work'd your wild poetic will!
Sir, you lack'd reverence, as I did,
Who in my impotence derided
The Artificer of storm and thunder,
   The great Self-Critic of Creation;
And now, like me, you've learn'd your blunder,
   You hug your doom and desolation.
Well, well, let gods and critics be,
Sit down a little space with me,
Comparing notes, our friends commending,
   Cursing our foes, this wintry night!
Come, though our strife is never ending,
   We've had our pleasure in the fight?
Not fearing Hell or hoping Heaven,
   We face the Elemental Flood;
Far better to be tempest-driven
   Than rot upon the harbour mud!'

'A ghost!'
       'A man!'
             'A poet's theme,
Woven of nightmare and of dream!'

'Nay, flesh and blood, sir – there's my hand
To prove it!'
          Laughing low, I took
His ring'd white hand in mine, and scanned
   His marble features like a book.
No sun-brown'd, wind-blown face, but one
Strange to the shining of the sun,
And sicklied o'er with sad moonlight
Beneath its ringlets black as night;
So young, and yet so old! – so still,

So callous and so coldly proud;
The eyes so bright, the cheeks as chill
    As some dead sleeper's in his shroud.
Gazing, I heard, beyond the sound
Of happy church-bells ringing round,
The murmur of the sleepless Sea
Stirring and breathing baleflly,
While Argus-eyed and strangely fair
    The wintry Heaven, stooping low,
Laid softly on its stormy hair,
With sighs of blessing and of prayer,
    Thin tremulous finger-tips of snow!

from

History of Cheadle

ROBERT PLANT

*It was 1881 when Robert Plant had his history of the once
agricultural town of Cheadle published. Much of his
description of customs came from an 1875 letter written from
South Devon by W.H. Keates, a former native of Cheadle. An
example of the guisers' mummery is given in the Christmas
St George play on page 89.*

In olden times the system of 'gooding' was carried on at Cheadle as well as in other parts of Staffordshire at Christmas time; and not only old men and women, but representatives from every poor family in the parish, made their rounds in quest of alms. During their peregrinations it was customary for the recipients of money to present to their benefactors a sprig of misletoe. It was also a practice here and at other places at one time for sums of money to be collected from the wealthy inhabitants and placed in the hands of the clergyman and churchwardens, who on the Sunday nearest St Thomas's Day distributed it in the vestry under the name of St Thomas's Dole.

'Whether the mummery of "guisers" (disguisers),' writes W.H. Keates, 'who went about the parish at Christmas when I was a boy, do so still, I do not know. The church singers and ringers went about the parish making collections for their services. Christmas waits or musicians, who for a month previously had gone about the parish giving night serenades, on Christmas Day and following days called on the parishioners with their music and made collections.' Opinions are much divided on the subject of waits. There are those who characterise nocturnal musicians as nuisances and their music as a barbarous relic of a byegone age. On the other hand, others profess to love 'sweet music in the stillness of the night.' The practice has not been discontinued altogether, nor is it a nuisance of an intolerable character, if a nuisance at all, at Cheadle, and will only die out altogether when a period is put to the almsgiving by which it has hitherto been supported.

Wassail Time

J.E. ROBERTS

'Written history has concerned itself with too few people, and precious few of them drawn from the ranks of ordinary folk'.
J.E. Roberts used this comment from a fellow enthusiast of Cannock Chase and its people to capture something of the passing of the old ways by publishing under the title, Bilberry Pie, *a recollection of local humour and language.*

'Ah was sittin' theer wi' me feet spragged up on th' chimdey piece, an' th' dog was layin' wi' 'is nose up th'ess'ole. Comfortable as two o'd biddies, nice an' cosy like. An' then we 'eard this noise. Couldn't meck it out: like th' moller-wowin's of a tumcat, wi' a weldin' 'eat on! Yo' should 'a' sin th' dog! Talk about 'ackles: they went up like Bumsted's collar, y' know, one o' them spit-overs . . .' Bill Stallman was talking to his club cronies.

'Twornt th' wailin' o' th' banshee?' asked Judder. 'Yo'r place aint bin up long enough t' be 'aunted. Sign o' jeth, they reckon.'

'Ah picked th' poker up, an' went out. An' what y' think? Twas kids, two skule kids – reckoned they'd bin carol singin'.'

'Was they swingin' it, like they do th' o'd dance tunes?' asked Judder.

'Swingin'? They was murderin' it!'

'Ah reckon as carol singin's like th' o'd grey mare: taint what it used t' be many long 'ears ago. Yo' jus' think back t' when we was kids.'

'Yo'm right theer, Jud,' chipped in Jim Baker. 'Skulin' wornt th' same then as now, but they med we sing at Chadsmer, like we was all linnets! Ah c'n still see Georgey Bigyed beltin' th' guts out o' th' joanna. Ar, an' beltin' our be'inds if we wornt up t' scratch!'

Judder's eyes twinkled with recollection: 'Yes, 'e'd 'ave eighty or p'raps ninety kids, all in one room: jam-packed like sardines. An' 'e'd be theer on 'is piano stool, like a tumtit on 'aystack, f'rocious as O'd Nick 'isself, meckin' we sing all about th' joys o' Christmas!' Judder cleared his throat: 'Y' know, Ah bet as we chaps could still do 'im a turn, if 'e was t' come back!

> 'Softly the night is sleeping,
> On Bethlehem's peaceful hill.
> Silent the shepherd watching
> Their gentle flocks are still.'

'Cruelty itself, Bigyed was, when th' mood took 'im,' said Jim. 'An' yet . . . Ah d'know . . . p'raps it was th'only road, wi' s'many on we in th' class. An' many on'm 'ellbats, at that!'

'Some taichers was wuss'n 'im,' said Judder. 'Teck Ernie Shaw, 'e'd got funny ways o' knockin' sense into kids, thraped'm at th' bottom end tryin' t' knock sense into th'r yeds. Funny way o' gooin' about it wornt it? Ah've known 'im lay kids down on th' desk an' 'ommer th'r backsides. Education, that was.'

'Would yo' chaps 'a' knowed Andy Powell,' asked Bill, changing the topic.

'Ah knowed two such chaps,' said Judder. 'One at Chadsmer, th'aberdasher, an' th'other from Green 'eath Road, up b' th' Fox.'

'That's th' one Ah mean, 'im from Hedgefud, worked at Ones. Well, one Christmas 'e'd done 'isself alright, laid a little barrel in. Some 'ow, 'is workmates got t' know. So they puts th'r yeds t'gether, wonderin' 'ow they might 'elp 'im t' see it

off! Well, they turns up at 'is backdoor, late on Christmas Eve, an' then lets fly:

'While shepherds watched th'r flocks b' night.'

Well, afore they'd really got tuned in, o'd Andy opens th' door, just a notch or two, an' they thought they was quids in! Afore they could meck any progress, though, Andy stopped'm: jus' lifted 'is fust finger, like. They all thought 'e was gooin' t' say summat special – an' 'e was: "Chaps, Ah know all about it bein' Christmas, but them next door, dunner: goo an' sing t' them!" An' wi' that, 'e slammed th' door!'

'Ah s'pose 'e thought charity'd better begin a-wum, even if it was only a little barrel,' said Judder, 'an' Ah dunner see as we c'n blame 'im, any more we c'n blame Bigyed!'

December 1962

The 1963 winter freeze-up meant a water queue for residents of Church Hill, Hednesford

Christmas Letter to Father

DAVID GARRICK

*The great English actor was educated at Lichfield Grammar
School. He also received instruction in Latin and Greek from Samuel
Johnson whom he later accompanied to London. Garrick was born
in Hereford during his father's posting to that city but the family
home was in Staffordshire's cathedral city. This letter was written to
the captain during his service with a regiment in Gibraltar.*

Lichfield
Decbr ye 23d 1734

Dear Sir,

We receiv'd a Letter from Mr Goddard and was vastly
surpriz'd to hear You had not receiv'd any Letter from us in
four Months, having I'm sure wrote four which you dont
make the least Mention of, and as I told Captn Goddard that
if the Ships were as certain Carriers, as we were Writers, You
would not I believe have any occasion to blame yr Son's
Neglect. In three of my last Letters I gave You an account of
my Mamma's Illness which confin'd her to her Room for four
Months, in which time she had several severe Relapses, and
was exceedingly bad that Morning she receiv'd Mr Goddard's
Letter which came very unseasonable, and was I'm sure no
forwarder of her Recovery. We were forc'd to call in Doctor

James who has been very diligent & carefull to recover her, so beg if you can procure any of the peruvian Bark he mentions in his Letter, you will let him have it. My Mamma's Disorder is a violent pain in her Hip & Thigh attended with a Fever on her Spirits, that Nothing gives her ease but opium, and she has been easy these three Weeks. We were in Hopes of seeing You this Xmas, and expect every Post News from London; My Mamma says she believes your presence would do more good than all the Physicians in Europe. Mr Morgan plagues Mr Arnold every Day who Promises very fair to do it this Day, and that Day so you may guess what expectations we live in, which if disappointed may cause a General indisposition throughout the Family. I wrote you word in one of my letters that Mr Bronkour was gone of for two thousand Pounds, & they say she'll sell coffee & Tea, &c, this Misfortune has caus'd grief to her Relations & Friends, Mr & Mrs Goddard are

Lichfield Cathedral in a winter 253 years after Garrick's letter

exceeding kind to them. Doctor James has so crested the Paper that I write upon it with the greatest Difficulty, so you must excuse Dear Sr the illshap'd Letters & crooked lines & impute them & other Faults to ye Doctor.

I am Sr Yr most Dutiful Son

David Garrick

P.S. I gave you an account in one of my letters (which I hope is receiv'd before this time) that my Mamma had receiv'd No Money from Moor the Chandler with all the particulars. The Family & Friends send their usual loves, Duties, Services &c wishing you a Merry Xmas & happy New Year, and I think we have about three Xmas boxes owing us, if not four.

A Hymn for Christmas Morning

MRS CRAIK

Best remembered for her 1857 novel, John Halifax, Gentleman, *Dinah Maria Mulock produced several volumes of poetry. The last of these entitled* Thirty Years Being Poems New and Old *was dedicated to her husband George Lillie Craik whom she had married in 1865. Her father was a Baptist minister in the Stoke area.*

1855

It is the Christmas time:
And up and down 'twixt heaven and earth,
In glorious grief and solemn mirth,
The shining angels climb.

And unto everything
That lives and moves, for heaven, on earth,
With equal share of grief and mirth,
The shining angels sing: –

'Babes new-born, undefiled,
In lowly hut, or mansion wide –
Sleep safely through this Christmas-tide
When Jesus was a child.

'O young men, bold and free,
In peopled town, or desert grim,
When ye are tempted like to Him,
"The man Christ Jesus" see.

'Poor mothers, with your hoard
Of endless love and countless pain –
Remember all her grief, her gain.
The Mother of the Lord.

'Mourners, half blind with woe,
Look up! One standeth in this place,
And by the pity of His face
The Man of Sorrows know.

'Wanderers in far countrie,
O think of Him who came, forgot.

To His own, and they received Him not –
Jesus of Galilee.

'O all ye who have trod
The wine-press of affliction, lay
Your hearts before His Heart this day –
Behold the Christ of God!'

Hartshill village, birthplace of Mrs Craik. Her father was a minister
here before the family went to live at Newcastle-under-Lyme

A Staffordshire Christmas

from

Adam Bede

GEORGE ELIOT

*Although her novels are more closely associated with
Warwickshire, George Eliot (Mary Ann Evans) did have
family connections with Staffordshire and visited her aunt at
Ellastone. This village becomes Hayslope in this extract from
her first and highly successful novel which was published in
1859.*

It was a busy time for Adam – the time between the
beginning of November and the beginning of February, and
he could see little of Hetty, except on Sundays. But a happy
time, nevertheless; for it was taking him nearer and nearer to
March, when they were to be married; and all the little
preparations for their new housekeeping marked the progress
towards the longed-for day. Two new rooms had been 'run up'
to the old house, for his mother and Seth were to live with
them after all. Lisbeth had cried so piteously at the thought of
leaving Adam, that he had gone to Hetty and asked her if, for
the love of him, she would put up with his mother's ways, and
consent to live with her. To his great delight, Hetty said, 'Yes;
I'd as soon she lived with us as not.' Hetty's mind was
oppressed at that moment with a worse difficulty than poor
Lisbeth's ways, she could not care about them. So Adam was
consoled for the disappointment he had felt when Seth had

come back from his visit to Snowfield and said 'it was no use – Dinah's heart wasna turned towards marrying.' For when he told his mother that Hetty was willing they should all live together, and there was no more need of them to think of parting, she said, in a more contented tone than he had heard her speak in since it had been settled that he was to be married, 'Eh, my lad, I'll be as still as th' ould tabby, an' ne'er want to do aught but th' offal work, as *she* wonna like t' do. An' then, we needna part the platters an' things, as ha' stood on the shelf together sin' afore thee wast born.'

There was only one cloud that now and then came across Adam's sunshine: Hetty seemed unhappy sometimes. But to all his anxious, tender questions, she replied with an assurance that she was quite contented and wished nothing different; and the next time he saw her she was more lively than usual. It might be that she was a little overdone with work and anxiety now, for soon after Christmas Mrs Poyser had taken another cold, which had brought on inflammation, and this illness had confined her to her room all through January. Hetty had to manage everything down-stairs, and half supply Molly's place too, while that good damsel waited on her mistress; and she seemed to throw herself so entirely into her new functions, working with a grave steadiness which was new in her, that Mr Poyser often told Adam she was wanting to show him what a good housekeeper he would have; but he 'doubted the lass was o'er-doing it – she must have a bit o' rest when her aunt could come down-stairs.'

This desirable event of Mrs Poyser's coming down-stairs happened in the early part of February, when some mild weather thawed the last patch of snow on the Binton Hills. On one of these days, soon after her aunt came down, Hetty went to Treddleston to buy some of the wedding things which were wanting, and which Mrs Poyser had scolded her for neglecting, observing that she supposed 'it was because they

'The slight hoar-frost had whitened the hedges in the early morning'

were not for th' outside, else she'd ha' bought 'em fast enough.'

It was about ten o'clock when Hetty set off, and the slight hoar-frost that had whitened the hedges in the early morning had disappeared as the sun mounted the cloudless sky. Bright February days have a stronger charm of hope about them than any other days in the year. One likes to pause in the mild rays of the sun, and look over the gates at the patient plough-horses turning at the end of the furrow, and think that the beautiful year is all before one. The birds seem to feel just the same: their notes are as clear as the clear air. There are no leaves on the trees and hedgerows, but how green all the grassy fields are! and the dark purplish brown of the ploughed earth and of the bare branches is beautiful too. What a glad world this looks like, as one drives or rides along the valleys and over the hills!

Staffordshire Christmas Carols

FREDERICK W. HACKWOOD

In his Staffordshire Customs, Superstitions & Folklore
Frederick Hackwood describes a number of Christmas activities
including carol-singing. Hackwood was a prolific local
historian producing many books about South Staffordshire
towns.

Carol Singing, like Wassailing, both customs of wide
observance, is honoured throughout Staffordshire, and both
customs could no doubt be traced to a pagan origin. As we
may recall, Virgil (Dryden's translation) has it anent the
winter festival of Saturn: –

> In jolly hymns they praise the god of wine,
> Whose earthen images adorn the pine,
> And there are hung on high in honour of the vine.

A NORTH STAFFORDSHIRE CAROL

Some years ago appeared in 'Notes and Queries' a curious
Christmas Carol, stated to have been taken down from the lips
of the boy who sang it, and who said he had learnt it from his
father, and had never seen it printed or written. It was

contributed by a correspondent in North Staffordshire, and is said to have been sung by the Morrice Dancers there to 'a wild and beautiful tune.' The composition shows it to be a specimen of pure folk-song: —

All the Bells in Paradise

Over yonder's a park, which is newly begun,
All bells in Paradise I heard them a-ring;
Which is silver on the outside, and gold within,
And I love sweet Jesus above all things.

And in that park there stands a hall,
All bells in Paradise I heard them a-ring;
Which is covered all over with purple and pall,
And I love sweet Jesus above all things.

And in that hall there stands a bed,
All bells in Paradise I heard them a-ring;
Which is hung all round with silk curtains so red,
And I love sweet Jesus above all things.

And in that bed there lies a knight,
All bells in Paradise I heard them a-ring;
Whose wounds they do bleed by day and by night,
And I love sweet Jesus above all things.

At that bed-side there lies a stone,
All bells in Paradise I heard them a-ring;
Which is our blessed Virgin Mary then kneeling on,
And I love sweet Jesus above all things.

At that bed's foot there lies a hound,
All bells in Paradise I heard them a-ring;

Carols at the Whittington Barracks, December 1970

Which is licking the blood as it daily runs down,
And I love sweet Jesus above all things.

At that bed's head there grows a thorn,
All bells in Paradise I heard them a-ring;
Which was never so blossomed since Christ was born,
And I love sweet Jesus above all things.

In the construction of this carol two characteristics of old-
time composition will be noted – the cumulative form of
narrative and the constant repetition of the refrain.
Altogether it rings true as a genuine emanation of the folk
mind.

A SOUTH STAFFORDSHIRE CAROL

Now compare it with a popular Christmas ditty sung by the children in South Staffordshire:–

The Sunny Bank

As I sat on the sunny bank,
As I sat on the sunny bank,
As I sat on the sunny bank,
    On Christmas Day in the morning.

I spied three ships come sailing by,
I spied three ships come sailing by,
I spied three ships come sailing by,
    On Christmas Day in the morning.

And who should be in these three ships,
And who should be in these three ships,
And who should be in these three ships,
    But Joseph and his fair lady.

O he did whistle, and she did sing,
And all the bells on earth did ring,
For joy our Saviour he was born
    On Christmas Day in the morning.

In medieval times church bells were rung for popular rejoicings; and the trees of Paradise were supposed to be hung with musical bells which were set ringing by the eternal breezes from the throne of God. In the popular mind, bells were ever an adjunct to the rendering of praise and glory, either to God or man.

Sonnet on 31st December 1782

ANNA SEWARD

*'The Swan of Lichfield' was the title bestowed on the then
young poetess who lived in the city from 1754 to her death in
1809. She was one of the glittering literati who gathered at
each other's homes for discussion on the latest political and
scientific ideas. Anna Seward's poetical works were edited in
three volumes by Walter Scott.*

Lo! the Year's final Day! – Nature performs
   Its obsequies with darkness, wind and rain;
   But man is jocund. – Hark! th' exultant strain
   From towers and steeples drowns the wintry storms!
No village spire but to the cots and farms,
   Right merrily, its scant and tuneless peal
   Rings round! – Ah! joy ungrateful! – mirth insane!
   Wherefore the senseless triumph, ye, who feel
This annual portion of brief life the while
   Depart for ever? – Brought it no dear hours
   Of health and night-rest? – none that saw the smile
On lips belov'd? – O! with as gentle powers
   Will the next pass? – Ye pause! – yet careless hear
   Strike these last clocks, that knell th' expiring year!

Arctic conditions in 1988 provided a happy time for this Lichfield
youngster

from

A Christmas Garland

SIR MAX BEERBOHM

A certain gentle humour emerges from the pen of the great essayist as he parodies the work of great writers such as Kipling, H.G. Wells, George Bernard Shaw, and of course Arnold Bennett. The satire heaped on the Five Towns followed the previous year's success with Zuleika Dobson *in 1911.*

SCRUTS

I

Emily Wrackgarth stirred the Christmas pudding till her right arm began to ache. But she did not cease for that. She stirred on till her right arm grew so numb that it might have been the right arm of some girl at the other end of Bursley. And yet something deep down in her whispered 'It is *your* right arm! And you can do what you like with it!'

She did what she liked with it. Relentlessly she kept it moving till it reasserted itself as the arm of Emily Wrackgarth, prickling and tingling as with red-hot needles in

every tendon from wrist to elbow. And still Emily Wrackgarth hardened her heart.

Presently she saw the spoon no longer revolving, but wavering aimlessly in the midst of the basin. Ridiculous! This must be seen to! In the down of dark hairs that connected her eyebrows there was a marked deepening of that vertical cleft which, visible at all times, warned you that here was a young woman not to be trifled with. Her brain despatched to her hand a peremptory message — which miscarried. The spoon wabbled as though held by a baby. Emily knew that she herself as a baby had been carried into this very kitchen to stir the Christmas pudding. Year after year, as she grew up, she had been allowed to stir it 'for luck.' And those, she reflected, were the only cookery lessons she ever got. How like Mother!

Mrs Wrackgarth had died in the past year, of a complication of ailments. Emily still wore on her left shoulder that small tag of crape which is as far as the Five Towns go in the way of mourning. Her father had died in the year previous to that, of a still more curious and enthralling complication of ailments. Jos, his son, carried on the Wrackgarth Works, and Emily kept house for Jos. She with her own hand had made this pudding. But for her this pudding would not have been. Fantastic! Utterly incredible! And yet so it was. She was grown-up. She was mistress of the house. She could make or unmake puddings at will. And yet she was Emily Wrackgarth. Which was absurd.

She would not try to explain, to reconcile. She abandoned herself to the exquisite mysteries of existence. And yet in her abandonment she kept a sharp look-out on herself, trying fiercely to make head or tail of her nature. She thought herself a fool. But the fact that she thought so was for her a proof of adult sapience. Odd! She gave herself up. And yet it was just by giving herself up that she seemed to glimpse sometimes her own inwardness. And these bleak revelations saddened

her. But she savoured her sadness. It was the wine of life to her. And for her sadness she scorned herself, and in her conscious scorn she recovered her self-respect.

It is doubtful whether the people of southern England have even yet realised how much introspection there is going on all the time in the Five Towns.

Visible from the window of the Wrackgarths' parlour was that colossal statue of Commerce which rears itself aloft at the point where Oodge Lane is intersected by Blackstead Street. Commerce, executed in glossy Doultonware by some sculptor or sculptors unknown, stands pointing her thumb over her shoulder towards the chimneys of far Hanbridge. When I tell you that the circumference of that thumb is six inches, and the rest to scale, you will understand that the statue is one of the prime glories of Bursley. There were times when Emily Wrackgarth seemed to herself as vast and as lustrously impressive as it. There were other times when she seemed to herself as trivial and slavish as one of those performing fleas she had seen at the Annual Ladies' Evening Fête organised by the Bursley Mutual Burial Club. Extremist!

She was now stirring the pudding with her left hand. The ingredients had already been mingled indistinguishably in that rich, undulating mass of tawniness which proclaims perfection. But Emily was determined to give her left hand, not less than her right, what she called 'a doing.' Emily was like that.

At mid-day, when her brother came home from the Works, she was still at it.

'Brought those scruts with you?' she asked, without looking up.

'That's a fact,' he said, dipping his hand into the sagging pocket of his coat.

It is perhaps necessary to explain what scruts are. In the daily output of every potbank there are a certain proportion of

flawed vessels. These are cast aside by the foreman, with a lordly gesture, and in due course are hammered into fragments. These fragments, which are put to various uses, are called scruts; and one of the uses they are put to is a sentimental one. The dainty and luxurious Southerner looks to find in his Christmas pudding a wedding-ring, a gold thimble, a threepenny-bit, or the like. To such fal-lals the Five Towns would say fie. A Christmas pudding in the Five Towns contains nothing but suet, flour, lemon-peel, cinnamon, brandy, almonds, raisins – and two or three scruts. There is a world of poetry, beauty, romance, in scruts – though you have to have been brought up on them to appreciate it. Scruts have passed into the proverbial philosophy of the district. 'Him's a pudden with more scruts than raisins to 'm' is a criticism not infrequently heard. It implies respect, even admiration. Of Emily Wrackgarth herself people often said, in reference to her likeness to her father, 'Her's a scrut o' th' owd basin.'

Jos had emptied out from his pocket on to the table a good three dozen of scruts. Emily laid aside her spoon, rubbed the palms of her hands on the bib of her apron, and proceeded to finger these scruts with the air of a connoisseur, rejecting one after another. The pudding was a small one, designed merely for herself and Jos, with remainder to 'the girl'; so that it could hardly accommodate more than two or three scruts. Emily knew well that one scrut is as good as another. Yet she did not want her brother to feel that anything selected by him would necessarily pass muster with her. For his benefit she ostentatiously wrinkled her nose.

'By the by,' said Jos, 'you remember Albert Grapp? I've asked him to step over from Hanbridge and help eat our snack on Christmas Day.'

Emily gave Jos one of her looks. 'You've asked that Mr Grapp?'

'No objection, I hope? He's not a bad sort. And he's considered a bit of a ladies' man, you know.'

She gathered up all the scruts and let them fall in a rattling shower on the exiguous pudding. Two or three fell wide of the basin. These she added.

'Steady on!' cried Jos. 'What's that for?'

'That's for your guest,' replied his sister. 'And if you think you're going to palm me off on to him, or on to any other young fellow, you're a fool, Jos Wrackgarth.'

The young man protested weakly, but she cut him short.

'Don't think,' she said, 'I don't know what you've been after, just of late. Cracking up one young sawny and then another on the chance of me marrying him! I never heard of such goings on. But here I am, and here I'll stay, as sure as my name's Emily Wrackgarth, Jos Wrackgarth!'

She was the incarnation of the adorably feminine. She was exquisitely vital. She exuded at every pore the pathos of her young undirected force. It is difficult to write calmly about her. For her, in another age, ships would have been launched and cities besieged. But brothers are a race apart, and blind. It is a fact that Jos would have been glad to see his sister 'settled' – preferably in one of the other four Towns.

She took up the spoon and stirred vigorously. The scruts grated and squeaked together around the basin, while the pudding feebly wormed its way up among them.

II

Albert Grapp, ladies' man though he was, was humble of heart. Nobody knew this but himself. Not one of his fellow clerks in Clither's Bank knew it. The general theory in Hanbridge was 'Him's got a stiff opinion o' hisself.' But this arose from what was really a sign of humility in him. He made the most of himself. He had, for instance, a way of his

own in the matter of dressing. He always wore a voluminous frock-coat, with a pair of neatly-striped vicuna trousers, which he placed every night under his mattress, thus preserving in perfection the crease down the centre of each. His collar was of the highest, secured in front with an aluminium stud, to which was attached by a patent loop a natty bow of dove-coloured sateen. He had two caps, one of blue serge, the other of shepherd's plaid. These he wore on alternate days. He wore them in a way of his own – well back from his forehead, so as not to hide his hair, and with the peak behind. The peak made a sort of half-moon over the back of his collar. Through a fault of his tailor, there was a yawning gap between the back of his collar and the collar of his coat. Whenever he shook his head, the peak of his cap had the look of a live thing trying to investigate this abyss. Dimly aware of the effect, Albert Grapp shook his head as seldom as possible.

On wet days he wore a mackintosh. This, as he did not yet possess a great-coat, he wore also, but with less glory, on cold days. He had hoped there might be rain on Christmas morning. But there was no rain. 'Like my luck,' he said as he came out of his lodgings and turned his steps to that corner of Jubilee Avenue from which the Hanbridge–Bursley trams start every half-hour.

Since Jos Wrackgarth had introduced him to his sister at the Hanbridge Oddfellows' Biennial Hop, when he danced two quadrilles with her, he had seen her but once. He had nodded to her, Five Towns fashion, and she had nodded back at him, but with a look that seemed to say 'You needn't nod next time you see me. I can get along well enough without your nods.' A frightening girl! And yet her brother had since told him she seemed 'a bit gone, like' on him. Impossible! He, Albert Grapp, make an impression on the brilliant Miss Wrackgarth! Yet she had sent him a verbal invite to spend Christmas in her own home. And the time had come. He was

on his way. Incredible that he should arrive! The tram must surely overturn, or be struck by lightning. And yet no! He arrived safely.

The small servant who opened the door gave him another verbal message from Miss Wrackgarth. It was that he must wipe his feet 'well' on the mat. In obeying this order he experienced a thrill of satisfaction he could not account for. He must have stood shuffling his boots vigorously for a full minute. This, he told himself, was life. He, Albert Grapp, was alive. And the world was full of other men, all alive; and yet, because they were not doing Miss Wrackgarth's bidding, none of them really lived. He was filled with a vague melancholy. But his melancholy pleased him.

In the parlour he found Jos awaiting him. The table was laid for three.

'So you're here, are you?' said the host, using the Five Towns formula. 'Emily's in the kitchen,' he added. 'Happen she'll be here directly.'

'I hope she's tol-lol-ish?' asked Albert.

'She is,' said Jos. 'But don't you go saying that to her. She doesn't care about society airs and graces. You'll make no headway if you aren't blunt.'

'Oh, right you are,' said Albert, with the air of a man who knew his way about.

A moment later Emily joined them, still wearing her kitchen apron. 'So you're here, are you?' she said, but did not shake hands. The servant had followed her in with the tray, and the next few seconds were occupied in the disposal of the beef and trimmings.

The meal began, Emily carving. The main thought of a man less infatuated than Albert Grapp would have been 'This girl can't cook. And she'll never learn to.' The beef, instead of being red and brown, was pink and white. Uneatable beef! And yet he relished it more than anything he had ever tasted.

This beef was her own handiwork. Thus it was because she had made it so. . . . He warily refrained from complimenting her, but the idea of a second helping obsessed him.

'Happen I could do with a bit more, like,' he said.

Emily hacked off the bit more and jerked it on to the plate he had held out to her.

'Thanks,' he said; and then, as Emily's lip curled, and Jos gave him a warning kick under the table, he tried to look as if he had said nothing.

Only when the second course came on did he suspect that the meal was a calculated protest against his presence. This a Christmas pudding? The litter of fractured earthenware was hardly held together by the suet and raisins. All his pride of manhood – and there was plenty of pride mixed up with Albert Grapp's humility – dictated a refusal to touch that pudding. Yet he soon found himself touching it, though gingerly, with his spoon and fork.

In the matter of dealing with scruts there are two schools – the old and the new. The old school pushes its head well over its plate and drops the scrut straight from its mouth. The new school emits the scrut into the fingers of its left hand and therewith deposits it on the rim of the plate. Albert noticed that Emily was of the new school. But might she not despise as affectation in him what came natural to herself? On the other hand, if he showed himself as a prop of the old school, might she not set her face the more stringently against him? The chances were that whichever course he took would be the wrong one.

It was then that he had an inspiration – an idea of the sort that comes to a man once in his life and finds him, likely as not, unable to put it into practice. Albert was not sure he could consummate this idea of his. He had indisputably fine teeth – 'a proper mouthful of grinders' in local phrase. But would they stand the strain he was going to impose on them? He could but try them. Without a sign of nervousness he

Longton chimneys

raised his spoon, with one scrut in it, to his mouth. This scrut
he put between two of his left-side molars, bit hard on it, and
– eternity of that moment! – felt it and heard it snap in two.
Emily also heard it. He was conscious that at sound of the
percussion she started forward and stared at him. But he did
not look at her. Calmly, systematically, with gradually
diminishing crackles, he reduced that scrut to powder, and
washed the powder down with a sip of beer. While he dealt
with the second scrut he talked to Jos about the Borough
Council's proposal to erect an electric power-station on the
site of the old gas-works down Hillport way. He was aware of
a slight abrasion inside his left cheek. No matter. He must be
more careful. There were six scruts still to be negotiated. He
knew that what he was doing was a thing grandiose, unique,
epical; a history-making thing; a thing that would outlive
marble and the gilded monuments of princes. Yet he kept his

head. He did not hurry, nor did he dawdle. Scrut by scrut, he ground slowly but he ground exceeding small. And while he did so he talked wisely and well. He passed from the power-station to a first edition of Leconte de Lisle's 'Parnasse Contemporain' that he had picked up for sixpence in Liverpool, and thence to the Midland's proposal to drive a tunnel under the Knype Canal so as to link up the main-line with the Critchworth and Suddleford loop-line. Jos was too amazed to put in a word. Jos sat merely gaping – a gape that merged by imperceptible degrees into a grin. Presently he ceased to watch his guest. He sat watching his sister.

Not once did Albert himself glance in her direction. She was just a dim silhouette on the outskirts of his vision. But there she was, unmoving, and he could feel the fixture of her unseen eyes. The time was at hand when he would have to meet those eyes. Would he flinch? Was he master of himself?

The last scrut was powder. No temporising! He jerked his glass to his mouth. A moment later, holding out his plate to her, he looked Emily full in the eyes. They were Emily's eyes, but not hers alone. They were collective eyes – that was it! They were the eyes of stark, staring womanhood. Her face had been dead white, but now suddenly up from her throat, over her cheeks, through the down between her eyebrows, went a rush of colour, up over her temples, through the very parting of her hair.

'Happen,' he said without a quaver in his voice, 'I'll have a bit more, like.'

She flung her arms forward on the table and buried her face in them. It was a gesture wild and meek. It was the gesture foreseen and yet incredible. It was recondite, inexplicable, and yet obvious. It was the only thing to be done – and yet, by gum, she had done it.

Her brother had risen from his seat and was now at the door. 'Think I'll step round to the Works,' he said, 'and see if they banked up that furnace aright.'

The Winter's Walk

SAMUEL JOHNSON

Although Johnson gave some thought to a collection of his poetry no edition of such a compilation was published in his lifetime. This particular poem originally appeared in the May edition of The Gentleman's Magazine *in 1747.*

Behold, my fair, where'er we rove,
What dreary prospects round us rise;
The naked hill, the leafless grove,
The hoary ground, the frowning skies!

Nor only thought the wasted plain,
Stern Winter in thy force confess'd;
Still wider spreads thy horrid reign,
I feel thy power usurp my breast.

Enlivening hope, and fond desire,
Resign the heart to spleen and care;
Scarce frighted love maintains her fire,
And rapture saddens to despair.

In groundless hope, and causeless fear,
Unhappy man! behold thy doom;
Still changing with the changeful year,
The slave of sunshine and of gloom.

'Stern winter' – a walk in the snow

Tir'd with vain joys, and falſe alarms,
With mental and corporeal ſtrife,
Snatch me, my Stella, to thy arms,
And ſcreen me from the ills of life.

Christmas Guisers

W. WELLS BLADEN

'If the folk-lore of Staffordshire is to be preserved, no time should be lost in collecting it' was emphasized by W. Wells Bladen when he read his Notes on the folk-lore of North Staffordshire, chiefly collected at Stone *presented as a paper in 1901 to a meeting of the North Staffordshire Naturalists Field Club and Archaeological Society. He described a number of Christmas customs, mostly of a general nature, but it is the presentation of the mummers' or guisers' play that is reproduced here in this extract.*

The Guisers' play of 'St George,' acted at Christmas, has probably been handed down from remote times. It was last performed in Stone in 1897. The players were dressed in any fantastic finery they could get – white and coloured calico, ribbons, and paper. They wore cardboard helmets, and were armed with wooden swords. The words as I give them were repeated to me from memory by James Hodgkiss. It is traditional. No one of those who played it here had ever seen it in either print or manuscript.

89

ST GEORGE

Characters:– *St George, Slasher, King of Egypt, Prince of Paradise, Hector, the Doctor, Bold Old Ben, Beelzebub*

PROLOGUE

I open the door, I enter in,
I hope your favour for to win;
Whether I rise, stand, or fall,
I'll do my best to please you all.
Stir up the fire to make a light,
To see these merry actors fight.
Room! Room! Ladies and gentlemen,
Give me gallant room to rhyme,
For I've come to show you some pretty acts,
All on this Christmas-time.
We're none of your ragged crew,
We're some of the royal trade,
We've crossed the seas your honours to please,
And now returned to old England again.

ACT I

(Enter St George)

St George
Here am I, St George, who from old England sprung,
My name is famous throughout this world and throne!
Many deeds and wonders have I made known!
I've made tyrants tremble on their throne.
I once followed a fair lady to a giant's gate,
Deep in dungeon to meet her fate;
Then I resolved, with true knight erranty,
To burst the door and set the prisoner free.
Then the giant he almost struck me dead,

But with my sword I took off his head.
If you can't believe the words I say,
Enter in, Slasher, thou gallant soldier,
And clear the way.

(Enter Slasher)

Slasher
I am a valiant soldier, and Slasher is my name;
With sword and buckler by my side,
I'm sure to play the game.
To force a fight with me I think you are not able,
For with my bright and glittering sword
I soon shall thee disable.

St George
Disable! disable! it is not in thy power,
For I soon shall thee devour;
So stand off, Slasher, let no more be said,
For if I draw my sword I'm safe to break thy head.

Slasher
How canst thou break my head,
When my head is made of iron?
My body's made of steel,
My hands and feet are knuckle and bone,
I'll challenge thee to feel.

(They fight, and Slasher is wounded)

(Enter King of Egypt)

King of Egypt
Alas! alas! my chiefest son is slain!
What shall I do to raise him up again?
Here he lies in the presence of you all,
I should loudly like for a doctor to be called.

A doctor! a doctor! five pounds for a doctor!
Ten pounds for a doctor! Is there ever a noble doctor to be found?

St George
I'll go and fetch one.

(*Enter Doctor*)

King of Egypt
Are you the doctor?

Doctor
Yes, as you can plainly see by my art and activity.

King of Egypt
What is thy fee to cure this man?

Doctor
My fee is ten pounds, but being as thou
Art an honest man, I'll only take five from thee.

King of Egypt (aside)
You'll be wonderful cunning if you get any.
How far hast thou travelled to be such a noble doctor?

Doctor
From Italy, Titatly, Germany, France, and Spain,
And now returned to cure diseases in old England again.

King of Egypt
So far and no farther?

Doctor
Oh yes, and a great deal further:
From the fireside to the cupboard door, upstairs and into bed.

King of Egypt
What diseases canst thou cure?

Doctor
All sorts.

King of Egypt
What is all sorts?

Doctor
The itch, the pitch, the palsy, and the gout.
If a man's got nineteen devils in his skull,
I can cast twenty of them out.
I have in my pocket crutches for lame ducks,
Spectacles for blind bumble bees,
And plaisters for broken-backed mice.
I cured St Harry of an agony almost 150 yards long,
And surely I can cure this poor man.

(To Slasher, giving him a drink)
Here, Jack, take a little pull out of my bottle
And let it run down thy throttle;
And if thou be'st not quite slain,
Rise up, Jack, and fight again.

Slasher
Oh, my back!

Doctor
What's amiss with thy back, Jack?

Slasher
My back is wounded, my heart is confounded,
To be knocked out of the life of seven senses into fourscore,

The like was never seen in old England before.
Then hark, St George! I hear the silver trumpets sounding,
Down yonder is the way,
So farewell, St George, I can no longer stay.   (*Dies*)

ACT II

St George

Here am I, St George, a noble champion bold;
And with my broad and glittering sword
I won ten thousand pounds in gold.
It was I who fought the fiery dragon, and its father I don't
     fear,
But through his heart I run my dreadful spear.
I've searched the world all round and round,

Christmas party at Colton, near Rugeley, in the early 1950s

And a man to equal me I've never found;
If you can't believe the word I say,
Enter in, Black Prince of Paradise! And clear the way!

(*Enter Black Prince of Paradise*)

Prince of Paradise
Here am I, Black Prince of Paradise, born of high renown,
Soon I'll fetch St George's courage down;
Before St George shall be deceived by me
St George shall die to all eternity.

St George
Stand off, thou black Morocco dog! or by my sword thou
   diest!
I'll make thy body full of holes and make thy buttons fly.

Prince of Paradise
Pull out thy purse to pay, draw out thy sword and slay,
For I mean to have some recompense before I go away.

St George
Now, Black Prince of Paradise, where hast thou been?
And pray what fine sights hast thou seen?
Dost think that no man of thy need
Dare such a Black as thou engage?
Lay down thy sword, take up a spear,
And I'll fight thee without dread or fear.
               (*They fight, and Prince of Paradise is killed*)
Now Black Prince of Paradise is dead,
And all his glory entirely fled;
Take him and give him to the flies,
And never more come near my eyes.

(*Enter King of Egypt*)

95

King of Egypt
I am the King of Egypt, who plainly doth appear;
I'm come to seek my son, my son and only heir.

St George
He's slain.

King of Egypt
Who did him slay? Who did him kill?

St George
I did him slay. I did him kill,
And on this ground his precious blood did spill.
Please you, my Lord, my honour to maintain,
Had you been here you might have shared the same.

(*Enter Hector*)

King of Egypt
Oh, Hector! Oh, Hector! Haste with speed,
For in my life I never stood more in need;
And don't stand there with sword in hand,
But use and fight at my command.

Hector
Yes, yes, my Lord, I will obey,
And with my sword I mean to win the day,
If that be he that does stand there,
That killed my master's son and heir,
Tho' he be sprung of royal blood,
I'll make it run enormous flood.

St George
Oh, Hector! Oh, Hector! Do not be so hot,
For in this room thou little think'st whom thou has got,

For I can deprive thee of this pride,
And lay thy anger to aside:
Slay thee, and cut thee as small as flies,
And send thee over the seas to make mincepies.

    Hector
How canst thou deprive me of my pride?
Or lay my anger to aside?
Since my head is made of iron,
My body's made of steel;
My hands and feet are knuckle and bone,
I'll challenge thee to feel.

                    (They fight, and Hector is wounded)
I am a gallant knight, and Hector is my name,
Many battles have I fought, and always won the game.
But from St George I received this wound,
Then hark, St George! I hear the silver trumpets sounding,
Down yonder is the way.
Farewell! St George, I can no longer stay.   *(Dies)*

                      (Enter Bold old Ben)

    Bold old Ben
Here comes past Bold old Ben!

    St George
Why, master, did I ever take thee to be my friend?

    Bold old Ben
Why, Jack, did I ever do thee any harm?

    St George
Thou proud saucy cockscomb, begone!

Bold old Ben
Cockscomb! I defy that name,
With a sword thou oughtest to be stabbed for the same.

St George
To be stabbed is the least I fear,
Appoint your time and place, I'll meet you there,
I'll cross the field at the hour of five,
And I'll meet you there, if thou be'st alive.

Bold old Ben
If you can't believe the word I say,
Enter in, Old Beelzebub, and clear the way.

(Enter Beelzebub)

Beelzebub
Here am I, Old Beelzebub,
And in my hand I carry my club,
And on my shoulder a dripping-pan,
I think myself a jolly old man.
Down in yonder meadows, where the birds sing funny,
Ladies and gentlemen, please fill my ladle with money.
My ladle's dumb and speak,
So fill it full, for St George's sake.

(Rings bell)

A ring, tink, tink, and a sup more drink,
And we'll make the old bell cry sound.

All dance   *Exeunt.*

from

Testament of Youth

VERA BRITTAIN

The First World War interrupted the Oxford studies of Newcastle-under-Lyme undergraduate, Vera Brittain, who was serving as a Voluntary Aid Detachment nurse at the time described in this extract. She did eventually marry in 1925 and her daughter, Shirley Williams, has carried forward her mother's struggle to achieve a high political profile for women.

Certainly the stage seemed perfectly set for his leave. Now that my parents had at last migrated temporarily to the Grand Hotel at Brighton, our two families were so near; the Matron had promised yet again that my own week's holiday should coincide with his, and even Edward wrote cheerfully for once to say that as soon as the actual date was known, he and Victor would both be able to get leave at the same time.

'Very wet and muddy and many of the communication trenches are quite impassable,' ran a letter from Roland written on December 9th. 'Three men were killed the other day by a dug-out falling in on top of them and one man was drowned in a sump hole. The whole of one's world, at least of one's visible and palpable world, is mud in various stages of solidity or stickiness. . . . I can be perfectly certain about the date of my leave by to-morrow morning and will let you know.'

And, when the final information did come, hurriedly written in pencil on a thin slip of paper torn from his Field Service note-book, it brought the enchanted day still nearer than I had dared to hope.

'Shall be home on leave from 24th Dec.–31st. Land Christmas Day. R.'

Even to the unusual concession of a leave which began on Christmas morning after night-duty the Matron proved amenable, and in the encouraging quietness of the winter's war, with no Loos in prospect, no great push in the west even possible, I dared to glorify my days – or rather my nights – by looking forward. In the pleasant peace of Ward 25, where all the patients, now well on the road to health, slept soundly, the sympathetic Scottish Sister teased me a little for my irrepressible excitement.

'I suppose you won't be thinking of going off and getting married? A couple of babies like you!'

It was a new and breath-taking thought, a flame to which Roland's mother – who approved of early marriages and believed that ways and means could be left to look after themselves far better than the average materialistic parent supposed – added fuel when she hinted mysteriously, on a day off which I spent in Brighton, that *this* time Roland might not be content to leave things as they were. . . . Suppose, I meditated, kneeling in the darkness beside the comforting glow of the stove in the silent ward, that during this leave we *did* marry as suddenly, as, in the last one, we became 'officially' engaged? Of course it would be what the world would call – or did call before the War – a 'foolish' marriage. But now that the War seemed likely to be endless, and the chance of making a 'wise' marriage had become, for most people, so very remote, the world was growing more tolerant. No one – not even my family now, I thought – would hold out against us, even though we hadn't a penny beyond our

Skating on Trentham Lake in February 1912

pay. What if, after all, we did marry thus foolishly? When the War was over we could still go back to Oxford, and learn to be writers – or even lecturers; if we were determined enough about it we could return there, even though – oh, devastating, sweet speculation – I might have had a baby.

I had never much cared for babies or had anything to do with them; before that time I had always been too ambitious, too much interested in too many projects, to become acutely conscious of a maternal instinct. But on those quiet evenings of night-duty as Christmas approached, I would come, half asleep, as near to praying as I had been at any time, even when Roland first went to France or in the days following Loos.

'Oh, God!' my half-articulate thoughts would run, 'do let us get married and let me have a baby – something that is Roland's very own, something of himself to remember him by

if he goes. . . . It shan't be a burden to his people or mine for a moment longer than I can help, I promise. I'll go on doing war-work and give it all my pay during the War – and as soon as ever the War's over I'll go back to Oxford and take my Finals so that I can get a job and support it. So *do* let me have a baby, dear God!'

The night before Christmas Eve, I found my ward transformed into the gay semblance of a sixpenny bazaar with Union Jacks, paper streamers, crinkled tissue lampshades and Christmas texts and greetings, all carried out in staggering shades of orange and vivid scarlet and brilliant green. In the cheerful construction of red paper bags, which I filled with crackers and sweets for the men's Christmas stockings, I found that the hours passed quickly enough. Clipping, and sewing, and opening packets, I imagined him reading the letter that I had written him a few days earlier, making various suggestions for meeting him, if he could only write or wire me beforehand, when the Folkestone train arrived at Victoria, and travelling down with him to Sussex.

'And shall I really see you again, and so soon?' it had concluded. 'And it will be the anniversary of the week which contained another New Year's Eve – and *David Copperfield*, and two unreal and wonderful days, and you standing alone in Trafalgar Square, and thinking of – well, what *were* you thinking of? When we were really both children still, and my connection with any hospital on earth was unthought-of, and your departure for the front merely the adventurous dream of some vaguely distant future date. And life was lived, at any rate for two days, in the Omar Khayyámesque spirit of

> *Unborn to-morrow and dead yesterday –*
> *Why fret about them if To-day be sweet?*

But we are going to better that – even that – *this* time. Au revoir.'

When I went to her office for my railway-warrant in the morning, the Matron smiled kindly at my bubbling impatience, and reminded me how lucky I was to get leave for Christmas. At Victoria I inquired what boat trains arrived on Christmas Day, and learnt that there was only one, at 7.30 in the evening. The risk, I decided, of missing him in the winter blackness of a wartime terminus was too great to be worth taking: instead, I would go straight to Brighton next morning and wait for him there.

As Christmas Eve slipped into Christmas Day, I finished tying up the paper bags, and with the Sister filled the men's stockings by the exiguous light of an electric torch. Already I could count, perhaps even on my fingers, the hours that must pass before I should see him. In spite of its tremulous eagerness of anticipation, the night again seemed short; some

Christmas party at Bagnall's Engine Works, Stafford, 1918

of the convalescent men wanted to go to early services, and that meant beginning temperatures and pulses at 3 a.m. As I took them I listened to the rain pounding on the tin roof, and wondered whether, since his leave ran from Christmas Eve, he was already on the sea in that wild, stormy darkness. When the men awoke and reached for their stockings, my whole being glowed with exultant benevolence; I delighted in their pleasure over their childish home-made presents because my own mounting joy made me feel in harmony with all creation.

At eight o'clock, as the passages were lengthy and many of the men were lame, I went along to help them to the communion service in the chapel of the college. It was two or three years since I had been to such a service, but it seemed appropriate that I should be there, for I felt, wrought up as I was to a high pitch of nervous emotion, that I ought to thank whatever God might exist for the supreme gift of Roland and the love that had arisen so swiftly between us. The music of the organ was so sweet, the sight of the wounded men who knelt and stood with such difficulty so moving, the conflict of joy and gratitude, pity and sorrow in my mind so poignant, that tears sprang to my eyes, dimming the chapel walls and the words that encircled them: 'I am the Resurrection and the Life: he that believeth in Me, though he were dead, yet shall he live: and whosoever liveth and believeth in Me shall never die.'

Directly after breakfast, sent on my way by exuberant good wishes from Betty and Marjorie and many of the others, I went down to Brighton. All day I waited there for a telephone message or a telegram, sitting drowsily in the lounge of the Grand Hotel, or walking up and down the promenade, watching the grey sea tossing rough with white surf-crested waves, and wondering still what kind of crossing he had had or was having.

When, by ten o'clock at night, no news had come, I

concluded that the complications of telegraph and telephone on a combined Sunday and Christmas Day had made communication impossible. So, unable to fight sleep any longer after a night and a day of wakefulness, I went to bed a little disappointed, but still unperturbed. Roland's family, at their Keymer cottage, kept an even longer vigil; they sat up till nearly midnight over their Christmas dinner in the hope that he would join them, and, in their dramatic, impulsive fashion, they drank a toast to the Dead.

The next morning I had just finished dressing, and was putting the final touches to the pastel-blue crêpe-de-Chine blouse, when the expected message came to say that I was wanted on the telephone. Believing that I was at last to hear the voice for which I had waited for twenty-four hours, I dashed joyously into the corridor. But the message was not from Roland but from Clare; it was not to say that he had arrived home that morning, but to tell me that he had died of wounds at a Casualty Clearing Station on December 23rd.

Lord Lichfield's Memories of Christmas Past

JANE SPIER

Shugborough, the magnificent country estate, is the ancestral home of the Earls of Lichfield. Today the county council administers this major visitor attraction on behalf of the National Trust. Here, spokesperson Jane Spier gives the Christmas recollections of the present earl, better known to the world as top photographer, Patrick Lichfield.

Christmas in the large country houses was without doubt a truly splendid and magical occasion – for the families that is.

Life 'backstairs' for the army of servants was quite a different matter. Preparations for the Christmas holidays would begin weeks in advance for staff in mansions like Shugborough, Lord Lichfield's ancestral home near Stafford. Lord Lichfield himself has many memories of Christmas past on this great estate.

As a small boy I particularly remember our Christmas celebrations in the Mansion . . . with housemaids up ladders, set astride a giant Pine in the Saloon. Under the tireless supervision of my Grandmother, a glorious

glittering picture unfolded, dancing and sparkling in the reflections of the fireside flames.

A sudden hush descended on the servants as a bell rang out announcing the arrival of FATHER CHRISTMAS . . . a rather rounded red figure appeared sporting a long white beard, laughing and chattering as he handed out gifts. As Father Christmas moved closer towards me, I began to suspect that this was indeed my Great Uncle, Colonel Keppall . . . the heavy smell of sherry was unmistakable . . .

The servants would gather in the saloon to be presented with gifts such as a length of material, from the family. The presents, though, would be handed to them by the butler of the household. The family would also give 'Christmas boxes' of money to tradesmen such as the grocer and the coal merchant.

Decorations usually took the form of festive foliage such as holly, ivy, mistletoe and laurel. The Victorians believed holly was lucky and that mistletoe would bring peace and harmony. A bower was made as a gateway to the grand rooms to greet guests as they arrived at the mansion. Fruit, ribbons and candles were used to decorate the fir trees. The effect was to remind children of the starlit heavens from which baby Jesus came.

Backstairs to the kitchens, where preparations for a variety of menus would have been completed for the family, house guests, the governess and the children of the family, and yet another menu for the servants. Even the humblest of Queen Victoria's subjects indulged in a special dinner of some kind by saving with the 'Goose Club' per week, so that by the time Christmas came around they would have enough for a goose and perhaps a bottle of spirits.

A typical Christmas menu at Shugborough would include

At Shugborough 'decorations usually took the form of festive foliage'

duck, beef, game, ham and chicken with a variety of sauces, vegetables, cakes and sweets. After the meat came the plum pudding. Although plum pudding was originally made with plums, by Victorian times people used raisins and currants instead. The pudding was nicknamed 'speckled cannonball', decorated with a sprig of holly and covered with burning brandy. To drink there would be port, mulled wine or wassail (hot spiced ale with apples).

Christmas and the Liberty of December

REVD R.W. ESSINGTON

Forty-seven years' service as a vicar of Shenstone was the lot of the Revd Robert William Essington during which time he compiled The Annals of Shenstone. *This old Etonian clergyman was also the author of a number of books on a range of topics from theology to income tax.*

Christmas-tide, and especially Christmas Day, was always a pleasant season at Waresley House, as also at Shenstone

Vicarage. The first was the mansion of one, not only a clergyman of distinction, but also a country gentleman of large fortune. The latter was a small Vicarage. At Waresley House there was alway a party of guests, the friends of the young people. These danced with the servants in the kitchen, and amongst themselves in the hall. Nothing of this sort could have been attempted at Shenstone Vicarage. But the poor widows came to a dinner, and were the special guests of Elizabeth Powner and Mary Black, both of whom had been from early youth trained by Mrs Essington to do the work of the house, and had become the livelong friends of the whole family. Then the ringers came to receive their annual present. In the kitchen the handbells were rung by them with great precision, after which cakes and ale appeared. The choir, if it had not preceded the ringers, followed them. These guests were treated with equal, although with a somewhat different sort of hospitality, suited to children. This was the kind of Christmas which prevails all over England, and which helps to promote that union between all sorts and conditions of men, on which the prosperity, not to say the existence, of a nation depends. And situated as the Vicar was in the close neighbourhood of Wall, where during 400 years at least a Roman Prætor ruled, he could not help thinking at Christmas of the December liberty which had preceded the Christian festival. Ancient in the days of Quintus Horatius Flaccus, it was still celebrated in accordance with custom – 'The Festival of Free Speaking!' Then everyone, old and young, rich and poor, master and slave, officer and private, said just what he liked to say. The sanctity of the season protected him, and no doubt much good was done. The Vicar often thought that such a December liberty might be useful, even in these days. Certainly it would be well if the clergy could be told gently, and without offence, that the times when a sermon formed the most attractive part of public worship are past. In former days

there were few books and fewer readers. Now both the one and the other abound. And the outcome of this change of circumstances is that a sermon, unless it be very good, must be very short. Nor is brevity, or as it is sometimes called a good finish, the only thing needed. The Dean of Worcester, amongst his stories, all of which were full of point, used to tell one of which, although he did not say so, he might have been the hero. It was as follows: – A young clergyman was required to preach before an ecclesiastical dignitary, and, with great folly, led up to a discussion of the sermon afterwards. In the course of this conversation he took occasion to say, 'I was not long, was I?' 'No,' replied the dignitary, 'you were not long. I admit that. So far you acted wisely.' On which the young clergyman added, 'I was quite determined not to be dull.' 'Oh,' rejoined the dignitary, 'but you were dull.' Members of trades unions, too, would greatly benefit by hearing a little free speaking. To prevent any man, or body of men, from working on such conditions as may appear suitable, is a tyranny. For themselves both masters and men may make such arrangements as they choose. But they must not force others into their bond against their judgment, whether that judgment be good or bad. This is the province of the State. And even the State will use this power as little as possible, for it may easily be abused. Some of the rich, too, might listen with advantage to home truths, especially in December. Let them eat the fat and drink the sweet by all means. All who are engaged in business earn their money by the sweat of the brain, which takes much more out of any human being than the sweat of the brow. Let them spend their wealth, and spend it freely. For the worst use which can be made of money in large sums is to hoard it. However foolishly it may be spent, as long as it is spent, it must benefit industrious people. But at all times, and more especially at Christmas, let the wealthy take care to send gifts to those for

whom nothing is prepared, remembering that the joy of the Lord is their strength. If anyone should be disposed to regard this chapter as a Christmas box on the ear, let him forgive it, as being the outcome of that December liberty which prevailed all over England, when the Imperial Romans constructed those roads, which are almost the only tokens of their long rule. These, and little more than these, the devastators who followed them have allowed to remain. In the parishes of Wall and of Shenstone nothing but the Watling Street Road speaks of Rome.

1947 drifts at Lloyd's corn merchants in Chadsmoor

from

Cola Monti

MRS CRAIK

Much of the work of Dinah Craik was for children, including
Cola Monti: a tale for boys. *The story concerns an Italian
boy, Niccolo Ficrentino del Monti, whom his Staffordshire
schoolmates nickname 'King Cole' or 'Cola'. He shows promise
as a caricaturist and goes to London in search of his artistic
fortune.*

HOW A BRIGHT MORNING WALK PRODUCED A
BRIGHT THOUGHT

'What, Cola, in bed still, this sunny Christmas morning!' said
Archibald, as he entered his friend's lodging.

'I don't see why I should get up,' was the answer. 'The
Museum is shut, so I can't go there as usual. I like staying in
bed, it is so still and quiet, one can doze and forget the world
and its cares.'

The disconsolate, weary tone revealed to Archy much that
he had before only suspected. Besides, the dreary aspect of the
fireless room, and the melancholy look of the pale sallow face
that lay on the pillow, confirmed the tale.

'Seppi, why don't you make haste and light the fire?' said
Cola, rather sharply. Then, recollecting himself: 'Oh, I forgot;
the lad is gone out for breakfast, if he can get it. You'll excuse

this, McKaye; all the world knows a poor artist is no Crœsus,'
he added with a bitter laugh.

Archy would not notice it. 'Come, Cola,' he said cheerfully,
'try and get up without a fire: you know the old rhyme –

> Early to bed and early to rise,
> Is the way to grow healthy, wealthy, and wise.'

'I shall never attain to the two latter; so I care little about
the first. The longer one lives, the more trouble one has; and
perhaps it is best to cut the matter short at once,' replied the
poor youth, whose state of mind was really pitiable. McKaye
penetrated it at once, and like a true friend went silently to
work, in order to remedy it. This time he abstained from
reading Cola a lecture; he knew it would not do. The boy
needed to be roused and cheered, not argued with; and the
only way was to draw him out of himself and his miseries.

'Cola, my dear fellow, this will never do; I can't be left to
spend a dull Christmas-day all by myself, at Mother Jones's.
Here is as bright a winter-day as ever shone out of the sky, and
I want to enjoy it with you. Let us both take a run out into
the country, up to Highgate or Hampstead. I'll give you a
Christmas dinner, in some nice quiet roadside inn, and we'll
walk home by star-light. There's a first-rate plan, eh! my
boy?'

'You are very good, but I should only bore you. Let me stay
here, Archy, and rest.'

'Well I call that rather too bad, after I have planned the
excursion all this week! Why, it would have been delicious,
just like our holidays together at the old doctor's! However, if
you will spoil my pleasure, you must. Only, I'll not be driven
out alone. I'll not stir an inch all day,' said Archy, settling
himself very composedly on one chair, with his feet on the
other. 'Now, you ill-natured fellow, go to sleep again, if you

like; I'll call you at dinner-time.'

Cola, miserable as he was, could not help laughing. 'Don't abuse me so, Archy; but indeed I am very dull and unhappy.' The laugh ended in a heavy sigh, and he put both his hands over his face.

McKaye rose up and took them away gently. 'Why did you not tell your friend Archy this, long before now? Isn't he as good as an elder brother to you, scoldings included? Come, now, be a good fellow and get up; and we'll talk over the misery; it will not look so black out in the open country as here. And we'll find some way to get out of it, may be,' said Archibald affectionately.

Cola obeyed him like a child. They stayed until Seppi came in and prepared breakfast, of which McKaye pretended to partake heartily, though he was not in the least hungry. And indeed the frugal, almost nauseous meal, was enough to drive hunger away. In another hour he and Cola were strolling arm-in-arm up the Highgate-road.

There is hardly a more beautiful walk anywhere near London than this same road. It looked so cheerful in the clear frosty morning, with its hawthorn and rose-hedges all besprinkled with crimson-berries, the ground crisp and pleasant underfoot, and overhead the bluest of winter skies. And then, at every turn of the winding and hilly road, came small beautiful 'bits,' as Cola, in artist-phrase entitled them; — tiny fragments, of landscape, not grand indeed, but very charming and refreshing, especially to one who for months had looked on nothing but bricks and mortar.

Cola's spirit rose. He leaned against the stile that leads from the hill nearest to Highgate, down a green meadow slope, to the Cemetery. He breathed the fresh morning air, and drank in with a painter's eye and soul the view before him. The full, bounding heart of youth beat once more in his bosom, and his eyes almost overflowed. Archy stood still

beside him, watching in glad silence the change that had come over the careworn face.

'How pleasant this is!' cried Monti at last. 'I begin to think the world is not so wretched after all; I have a great mind to give it another trial. Don't smile, Archy,' continued he; 'but if you knew what miserable wicked thoughts I have had of late' ——

'Why so?'

'Because I am disappointed in all I attempt. It is very hard to wait day after day, and have no chance of anything but starvation; and sometimes Seppi and I have not been so far off that already.'

'My poor Cola, and I never knew it!'

'Of course not, and you would not have known it now, only I am so down-hearted and foolish, and you are so kind.'

'This will never do, my dear lad; I can't stand by and see you breaking your heart and pining away in this quiet composed fashion, until you give me the satisfaction of finding you a comfortable home out there,' answered McKaye, pointing to the Highgate cemetery before them, and making a desperate attempt at comicality, which he generally did when much affected. 'Just throw some light on the subject, will you? let me into your matters a little. We can hold a cabinet-council very conveniently on this stile. Begin, my boy!'

And partly with seriousness, partly by a little harmless jesting, Archibald succeeded in arriving at the true state of affairs. He walked on thoughtfully for a little, and then said, ——

'Cola, it strikes me you are on the wrong tack. Instead of waiting until people find you employment, (I beg your pardon for applying the term to such a grand thing as Art,) you ought to look for it yourself. Don't trust any longer to these great folk; stand up boldly on your own account. You

are a very clever fellow, and I'll never believe but that such talent as yours will make its way.'

'Much obliged to you, Archy, for your good opinion; but how am I to convert talent into money? I am not yet skilful in painting; nobody would buy my daubs, and it torments me even to have to disgrace myself by selling such rubbish, when, with a little experience, I might do something creditable. What am I to turn to, in order to find bread, while I work out the powers which I feel I have within me?'

'That is just what I have been considering. Now, here is my plan. You know all the world is mad for illustrated books, and I am sure I have seen designs of yours enough to paper a room. (Don't look so vexed, dear Cola, you know my ways.) With your fertile imagination and ready hand, why not turn wood-draughtsman?'

'Wood-draughtsman!' echoed the young artist, rather surprised, and perhaps a little humiliated.

'Yes; it is an excellent profession, and will serve until better times come. Besides, you might keep on with the painting still.'

'But I know no Art-publishers; and have no introductions.'

'Who cares for introductions? My dear fellow, stand on your own feet; trust to your own talents. Never fear but they will find their proper level. Go from one publisher to another, as a youth like you may do without lowering the dignity of Art. Take your portfolio under your arm, and your own genius will be your best introduction. For you have genius, Cola, and I know and feel it, though I do laugh at you sometimes. You'll get work, never fear. Take my word for it, that a clever fellow like you need never starve, if to his talent he only adds a little common sense, so as to show him how to use it. People will find out his value, and treat him kindly too; for the world, like a certain other individual of whom I don't think it proper to speak, is by no means as black as it's painted.'

Cola laughed merrily. 'You are a wise fellow, Archy, though your wisdom comes out chiefly in a joke. I'll think over what you say.'

'And act upon it, Cola?'

'I will; there's my hand as a pledge. I feel brave already – could face all the Art-publishers in London. Let me see; to-morrow is Saturday; and these English people eat and drink so much on Christmas-day, that they are never thoroughly awake the day after. But on Monday I will set about your scheme. Dear Archy, how much lighter you have made my heart!'

They took the homeward walk by starlight, as McKaye had planned, and the quiet beautiful night drew their hearts nearer together. Their talk comprehended the deepest feelings of both; Cola's hopes of the future, with all his artist-dreams; – and the far-off cottage near Aberdeen, whither all the strong home-affections of the young Scotsman ever turned.

'You shall go there some time, Cola,' said Archy. 'I long to show you my father and mother, and the five boys – and my little sister Jessie. She's grown a woman now though. You shall take all their likenesses in a family group. But by then you will have got far above portrait-painting, and be working at grand historical pictures, with figures ten feet high – *à la* Michel Angelo.'

Cola's cheerful laugh again rang through the clear frosty air. He had recovered that lost talisman, without which youth – especially youth allied with genius – cannot long exist. He could once more walk through the world erect, for he had hope in his bosom.

from

The Life of Samuel Johnson

JAMES BOSWELL

Much of the continued popularity of Samuel Johnson as a wit and man of literature is due in part to The Life of Samuel Johnson *with his correspondence and conversations published in 1791 by his friend and biographer James Boswell. This exchange of Christmas greetings recalled here was typical of their friendship and came five years after Boswell's announced intention to produce such a biography.*

TO JAMES BOSWELL, ESQ.

Dear Sir,

This is the time of the year in which all express their good wishes to their friends, and I send mine to you and your family. May your lives be long, happy, and good. I have been much out of order, but, I hope, do not grow worse.

The crime of the school master whom you are engaged to prosecute is very great, and may be suspected to be too common. In our law it would be a breach of the peace and a misdemeanour: that is, a kind of indefinite crime, not capital,

but punishable at the discretion of the Court. You cannot want matter: all that needs to be said will easily occur.

Mr Shaw, the author of the Gaelic Grammar, desires me to make a request for him to Lord Eglintoune, that he may be appointed Chaplain to one of the new-raised regiments.

All our friends are as they were; little has happened to them of either good or bad. Mrs Thrale ran a great black hair-dressing pin into her eye; but by great evacuation she kept it from inflaming, and it is almost well. Miss Reynolds has been out of order, but is better. Mrs Williams is in a very poor state of health.

If I should write on, I should, perhaps, write only complaints, and therefore I will content myself with telling you, that I love to think on you, and to hear from you; and that I am, dear Sir,

Yours faithfully,
Sam. Johnson

December 27, 1777

TO DR SAMUEL JOHNSON

Edinburgh, Jan. 8, 1778

Dear Sir,

Your congratulations upon a new year are mixed with complaint: mine must be so too. My wife has for some time been very ill, having been confined to the house these three months by a severe cold, attended with alarming symptoms.

[Here I gave a particular account of the distress which the person upon every account most dear to me suffered; and of the dismal state of apprehension in which I now was: adding, that I never stood more in need of his consoling philosophy.]

Did you ever look at a book written by Wilson, a Scotchman, under the Latin name of *Volusenus*, according to the custom of literary men at a certain period. It is entitled 'De Animi Tranquillitate.' I earnestly desire tranquillity. *Bona res quies*; but

I fear I shall never attain it: for, when unoccupied, I grow gloomy; and occupation agitates me to feverishness.

I am, dear Sir,

Your most affectionate humble servant,

James Boswell

TO JAMES BOSWELL, ESQ.

Dear Sir,

To a letter so interesting as your last, it is proper to return some answer, however little I may be disposed to write.

Your alarm at your lady's illness was reasonable, and not disproportionate to the appearance of the disorder. I hope your physical friend's conjecture is now verified, and all fear of a consumption at an end: a little care and exercise will then restore her. London is a good air for ladies; and if you bring her hither, I will do for her what she did for me – I will retire from my apartments for her accommodation. Behave kindly to her, and keep her cheerful.

You always seem to call for tenderness. Know, then, that in the first month of the present year I very highly esteem and very cordially love you. I hope to tell you this at the beginning of every year as long as we live; and why should we trouble ourselves to tell or hear it oftener?

Tell Veronica, Euphemia, and Alexander, that I wish them, as well as their parents, many happy years.

You have ended the negro's cause much to my mind. Lord Auchinleck and dear Lord Hailes were on the side of liberty. Lord Hailes's name reproaches me; but if he saw my languid neglect of my own affairs, he would rather pity than resent my neglect of his. I hope to mend, *ut et mihi vivam et amicis.*

I am, dear Sir, yours affectionately,

Sam. Johnson

January 24, 1778

from

The Wandering Jew:
A Christmas Carol
ROBERT WILLIAMS BUCHANAN

'To my dear father Robert Buchanan poet and social missionary
this Christmas gift. Christmas 1892' is the dedication in the
book. Perhaps the father who was a declared securalist
appreciated his son's treatment of the medieval legend of the Jew
whose insult to Jesus condemned him to walk the face of the
Earth till Judgement Day. Aside from his poetry the younger
Robert wrote a number of novels and plays, many successful in
their time but now forgotten.

As in the City's streets I wander'd late,
Bitter with God because my wrongs seem'd great,
Chiller at heart than the bleak winds that blew
Under the star-strewn voids of steel-bright blue,
Sick at the silence of the Snow, and dead
To the white Earth beneath and Heaven o'erhead,
I heard a voice sound feebly at my side
In hollow human accents, and it cried
'For God's sake, mortal, let me lean on thee!'
And as I turn'd in mute amaze to see
Who spake, there flew a whirlwind overhead
In which the lights of Heaven were darkenèd,

Shut out from sight or flickering sick and low
Like street-lamps when a sudden blast doth blow;
But I could hear a rustling robe wind-swept
And a faint breathing; then a thin hand crept
Into mine own, clammy and cold as clay!

'Twas on that Night which ushereth in Christ's Day.
The winds had winnowèd the drifts of cloud,
But the white fall had ceased. There, pale and proud,
In streets of stone empty of life, while Sleep
In silvern mist hung beautiful and deep
Over the silent City even as breath,
I mused on God and Man, on Life and Death,
And mine own woe was as a glass wherein
I mirror'd God's injustice and Man's sin.
And so, remembering the time, I sneer'd
To think the mockery of Christ's birth-tide near'd,
And pitying thought of all the blinded herd
Who eat the dust and ashes of the Word,
Holding for all their light and all their good
The Woeful Man upon the Cross of wood;
And bitterly to mine own heart I said,
'In vain, in vain, upon that Cross he bled!
In vain he swore to vanquish Death, in vain
He spake of that glad Realm where he should reign!
Lo, all his promise is a foolish thing,
Flowers gathered by a child and withering
In the moist hand that holdeth them; for lo!
Winter hath come, and on his grave the snow
Lies mountain-deep; and where he sleeping lies
We too shall follow soon and close our eyes
Unvex'd by dreams. The golden Dream is o'er,
And he whom Death hath conquer'd wakes no more!'

Even then I heard the desolate voice intone,
And the thin hand crept trembling in my own,
And while my heart shut sharp in sudden dread
Against the rushing blood, I murmurèd
'Who speaks? who speaks?' Suddenly in the sky
The Moon, a luminous white Moth, flew by,
And from her wings silent and mystical
Thick rays of vitreous dust began to fall,
Illuming Earth and Heaven; when I was 'ware
Of One with reverend silver beard and hair
Snow-white and sorrowful, looming suddenly
In the new light like to a leafless Tree
Hung round with ice and magnified by mist
Against a frosty Heaven! But ere I wist
Darkness return'd, the splendour died away,
And all I felt was that thin hand which lay
Fluttering in mine!
                    Then suddenly again
I heard the tremulous voice cry out in pain
'For God's sake, mortal, let me lean on thee!'
And peering thro' the dimness I could see
Snows of white hair blowing feebly in the wind;
And deeply was I troubled in my mind
To see so ancient and so weak a Wight
At the cold mercy of the storm that night,
And said, while 'neath his wintry load he bent,
'Lean on me, father!' adding, as he leant
Feebly upon me, wearied out with woe,
'Whence dost thou come? and whither dost thou go?'

Vera's Second Christmas Adventure

ARNOLD BENNETT

This second story about Vera Cheswardine comes as the first one did from a number of short stories published under the title The Grim Smile of the Five Towns. *Here Bennett exercised his writing craft as an observer of human nature.*

I

Curious and strange things had a way of happening to Vera – perhaps because she was an extremely feminine woman. But of all the curious and strange things that ever did happen to Vera, this was certainly the strangest and the most curious. It makes a somewhat exasperating narrative, because the affair ended – or, rather, Vera caused it to end – on a note of interrogation. The reader may, however, draw consolation from the fact that, if he is tormented by an unanswerable query, Vera herself was much more tormented by precisely the same query.

Two days before Christmas, at about three o'clock in the afternoon, just when it was getting dusk and the distant smoke-pall of the Five towns was merging in the general

greyness of the northern sky, Vera was sitting in the bow-window of the drawing-room of Stephen Cheswardine's newly-acquired house at Sneyd; Sneyd being the fashionable suburb of the Five Towns, graced by the near presence of a countess. And as the slim, thirty-year-old Vera sat there, moody (for reasons which will soon appear), in her charming teagown, her husband drove up to the door in the dogcart, and he was not alone. He had with him a man of vigorous and dashing appearance, fair, far from ugly, and with a masterful face, keen eyes, and most magnificent furs round about him. At sight of the visitor Vera's heart did not exactly jump, but it nearly jumped.

Presently, Stephen brought his acquaintance into the drawing-room.

'My wife,' said Stephen, rubbing his hands. 'Vera, this is Mr Bittenger, of New York. He will give us the pleasure of spending the night here.'

And now Vera's little heart really did jump.

She behaved with the delicious wayward grace which she could always command when she chose to command it. No one would have guessed that she had not spoken to Stephen for a week.

'I'm most happy – most happy,' said Mr Bittenger, with a marked accent and a fine complimentary air. And obviously he was most happy, Vera had impressed him. There was nothing surprising in that. She was in the fulness of her powers in that direction.

It is at this point – at the point of the first jumping of Vera's heart – that the tale begins to be uncanny and disturbing. Thus runs the explanation.

During the year Stephen had gradually grown more and more pre-occupied with the subject of his own health. The earthenware business was very good, although, of course, manufacturers were complaining just as usual. Trade, indeed,

flourished to such an extent that Stephen had pronounced himself to be suffering from nervous strain and overwork. The symptoms of his malady were chiefly connected with the assimilation of food; to be brief, it was dyspepsia. And as Stephen had previously been one of those favoured people who can eat anything at any hour, and arise in the best of health the next day, Stephen was troubled. At last – about August, when he was obliged to give up wine – he had suddenly decided that the grimy air of the Five Towns was bad for him, and that the household should be removed to Sneyd. And removed to Sneyd it accordingly was. The new house was larger and more splendid even than the Cheswardine abode at Bursley. But Vera did not like the change. Vera preferred the town. Nevertheless, she could not openly demur, since Stephen's health was supposed to be at stake.

During the autumn she was tremendously bored at Sneyd. She had practically no audience for her pretty dresses, and her friends would not flock over from Bursley because of the difficulty of getting home at night. Then it was that Vera had the beautiful idea of spending Christmas in Switzerland. Some one had told her about a certain hotel called The Bear where, on Christmas Day, never less than a hundred well-dressed and wealthy English people sat down to an orthodox Christmas dinner. The notion enchanted her. She decided, definitely, that she and Stephen should do their Christmassing at The Bear, wherever The Bear was. And as she was fully aware of the power of her capricious charm over Stephen, she regarded the excursion as arranged before she had broached it to him.

Stephen refused. He remarked bitterly that the very thought of a mince-tart made him ill; and that he hated 'abroad.'

Vera took her defeat badly.

She pouted. She sulked. She announced that, if she was

not to be allowed to do her Christmassing at The Bear, she would not do it anywhere. She indicated that she meant to perish miserably of *ennui* in the besotted dulness of Sneyd, and that no Christmas-party of any kind should occur in *her* house. She ceased to show interest in Stephen's health. She would not speak. In fact, she went too far. One day, in reply to her rude silence, Stephen said: 'Very well, child, if that's your game, I'll play it with you. Except when other people are present, not a word do I speak to you until you have first spoken to me.'

She knew he would abide by that. He was a monster. She hated him. She loathed him (so she said to herself).

That night, in the agony of her distress, she had dreamed a dream. She dreamed that a stranger came to the house. The details were vague, but the stranger had travelled many

1899 Christmas window display at Marson's Greengate Street, Stafford

128

miles over water. She could not see him distinctly, but she knew that he was quite bald. In spite of his baldness, he inspired her with sympathy. He understood her, praised her costumes, and treated a woman as a woman ought to be treated. Then, somehow or other, he was making love to her, the monster Stephen being absent. She was shocked by his making love to her, and she moved a little further off him on the sofa (he had sat down by her on a vague sort of sofa in a vague sort of room); but still she was thrilled, and she could not feel as wicked as she felt she ought to feel. Then the dream became hazy; it became hazy at the interesting point of her answer to the love-making. A later stage was very clear. Something was afoot between the monster Stephen and the stranger in the dining-room, and she was locked out of the dining-room. It was Christmas night. She knocked frantically at the door, and at last forced it open, and Stephen was lying in the middle of the floor; the table had been pushed into a corner. 'I killed him quite by accident,' said the stranger affably. And then he seized her by the hand and ruthlessly dragged her away, away, away; and they travelled in trains and ships and trains, and they came to a very noisy, clanging sort of city – and Vera woke up. It had been a highly realistic dream, and it made a deep impression on Vera.

Can one wonder that Vera's heart, being a superstitious little heart, like all our hearts, should leap when the very next day Stephen turned up with a completely unexpected stranger from New York? Of course, dreams are nonsense! Of course! Still——

She did not know whether to rejoice or mourn over the fact that Mr Bittenger was not bald. He was decidedly un-bald; he had a glorious shock of chestnut hair. That hair of his naturally destroyed any possible connection with the dream. None the less the coincidence was bizarre.

II

That evening, before dinner, Vera, busy in her chamber beautifying her charms for the ravishment of men from New York, waited with secret anxiety for the arrival of Stephen in his dressing-room. And whereas she usually closed the door between the bedroom and the dressing-room, on this occasion she carefully left it wide open. Stephen came at last. And she waited, listening to his movements in the dressing-room. Not a word! She made brusque movements in the bedroom to attract his attention; she even dropped a brush on the floor. Not a word! After a few moments, she actually ventured into the dressing-room. Stephen was wiping his face, and he glanced at her momentarily over the towel, which hid his nose and mouth. Not a word! And how hard was the monster's glance! She felt that Stephen was one of your absurd literal persons. He had said that he would not speak to her until she had first spoken to him – that was to say in private – public performances did not count. And he would stick to his text, no matter how deliciously she behave!

She left the dressing-room in haste. Very well! Very well! If Stephen wished for war, he should have it. Her grievance against him grew into something immense. Before, it had been nothing but a kind of two-roomed cottage. She now erected it into a town hall, with imposing portals, and many windows and rich statuary, and suite after suite of enormous rooms, and marble staircases, and lifts that went up and down. She wished she had never married him. She wished that Mr Bittenger *had* been bald.

At dinner everything went with admirable smoothness. Mr Bittenger sat betwixt them. And utmost politeness reigned. In their quality of well-bred hosts, they both endeavoured to keep Mr Bittenger at his ease despite their desolating quarrel; and they entirely succeeded. As the champagne disappeared

(and it was not Stephen that drank it), Mr Bittenger became more than at his ease. He was buyer for an important firm of earthenware dealers in New York (Vera had suspected as much – these hospitalities to American buyers are an essential part of business in the Five Towns), and he related very drolly the series of chances or mischances that had left him stranded in England at that season so unseasonable for buying. Vera reflected upon the series of chances or mischances, and upon her dream of the man from over the long miles of water. Of course, dreams are nonsense. . . . But still——

The conversation passed to the topic of Stephen's health, as conversations in Stephen's house had a habit of doing. Mr Bittenger listened with grave interest.

'I know, I know!' said Mr Bittenger. 'I used to be exactly the same. I guess I understand how you feel – *some!* Don't I?'

'And you are cured?' Stephen demanded, eagerly, as he nibbled at dry toast.

'You bet I'm cured!' said Mr Bittenger.

'You must tell me about that,' said Stephen, and added, 'some time to-night.' He did not care to discuss the bewildering internal economy of the human frame at his dinner-table. There were details . . . and Mr Bittenger was in a mood that it was no exaggeration to describe as gay.

Shortly afterwards, there arose a discussion as to their respective ages. They coquetted for a few moments, as men invariably will, each diffident about giving away the secret, each asserting that the other was younger than himself.

'Well,' said Mr Bittenger to Vera, at length, 'what age should you give me?'

'I – I should give you five years less than Stephen,' Vera replied.

'And may I ask just how old you are?' Mr Bittenger put the question at close range to Stephen, and hit him full in the face with it.

Helping to clear the snow in Price Street, Cannock, 1963

'I'm forty,' said Stephen.

'So am I!' said Mr Bittenger.

'Well, you don't look it,' said Stephen.

'Sure!' Mr Bittenger admitted, pleased.

'My husband's hair is turning grey,' said Vera, 'while yours——'

'Turning grey!' exclaimed Mr Bittenger. 'I wish mine was. I'd give five thousand dollars to-day if mine was.'

'But why——?' Vera smiled.

'Look here, my dear lady,' said Mr Bittenger, in a peculiar voice, putting down his glass.

And with a swift movement he lifted a wig of glorious chestnut hair from his head – just lifted it for an instant, and dropped it. The man was utterly and completely bald.

III

Vera did nothing foolish. She neither cried, screamed, turned deadly pale, clenched her fragile hands, bit her lips till the blood came, smashed a wine-glass, nor fell with a dull thud senseless to the floor. Nevertheless, she was extremely perturbed by this astounding revelation of Mr Bittenger's. Of course, dreams are nonsense. But still—— The truth is, one tries to believe that dreams are nonsense, and up to a certain point one may succeed in believing. But it seemed to Vera that circumstances had passed that point. She could not but admit, also, that if the dream went on being fulfilled, within forty-eight hours Mr Bittenger would have made love to her, and would have killed her husband.

She was so incensed against Stephen that she really could not decide whether she wanted the dream to be fulfilled or not. No one would have imagined that that soft breast could conceal a homicidal thought. Yet so it was. That pretty and delightful woman, wandering about in the edifice of her

terrific grievance against Stephen, could not say positively to herself that she would not care to have Stephen killed as a punishment for his sins.

After dinner, she found an excuse for retiring. She must think the puzzle out in solitude. Matters were really going too far. She allowed it to be understood that she was indisposed. Mr Bittenger was full of sorrow and sympathy. But did Stephen show the slightest concern? Stephen did not. She went up-stairs, and she meditated, stretched on the sofa at the foot of the bed, a rug over her knees and the fire glinting on her face. Yes, it was her duty as a Christian, if not as an outraged wife, to warn Stephen that the shadow of death was creeping up behind him. He ought at least to be warned. But how could she warn him? Clearly she could not warn him in the presence of Mr Bittenger, the prospective murderer. She would, therefore, have to warn him when they were alone. And that meant that she would have to give way in the great conjugal sulking match. No, never! It was impossible that she should give way there! She frowned desperately at the leaping flames, and did ultimately decide that Stephen's death was preferable to her defeat in that contest. Of such is human nature.

After all, dreams were nonsense.

Surely Stephen would come up-stairs to inquire about her health, her indisposition? But no! He came not. And, as he continued not to come, she went down-stairs again and proclaimed that she was better.

And then she learned that she had been worrying herself to no purpose whatever. Mr Bittenger was leaving on the morrow, the morrow being Christmas Eve. Stephen would drive him to Bursley in the morning. He would go to the Five Towns Hotel to get his baggage, and catch the Liverpool express at noon. He had booked a passage on the *Saxonia*, which sailed at three-thirty o'clock. Thus he would spend his

Hanley market-place in the early 1900s

Christmas at sea; and, spending his Christmas at sea, he could not possibly kill Stephen in the village of Sneyd on Christmas night.

Relief! And yet a certain vague regret in the superstitious little heart! The little heart went to bed again. And Stephen and the stranger stayed up talking very late – doubtless about the famous cure.

The leave-taking the next morning increased the vague regret. Mr Bittenger was the possessor of an attractive individuality, and Vera pondered upon its attractiveness far into the afternoon. How nicely Mr Bittenger had thanked her for her gracious hospitality – with what meaning he had charged the expression of his deep regret at leaving her!

After all, dreams *were* nonsense.

She was sitting in the bow-window of the drawing-room, precisely as she had been sitting twenty-four hours previously,

when whom should she see, striding masculinely along the drive towards the house, but Mr Bittenger?

This time she was much more perturbed even than she had been by the revelation of Mr Bittenger's baldness.

After all——

She uprose, the blood having rushed to her head, and retreated she knew not whither, blindly, without a purpose. And she found herself in a little morning-room, which was scarcely ever used, at the end of the hall. She had not shut the door. And Mr Bittenger, having been admitted by a servant, caught sight of her, and breezily entered her retreat, clad in his magnificent furs.

And as he doffed the furs, he gaily told her what had happened. Owing to difficulties with the Cheswardine mare on the frosty, undulating road between Sneyd and Bursley, and owing to delays with his baggage at the Five Towns Hotel, he had just missed the Liverpool express, and, therefore, the steamer also. He had returned to Stephen's manufactory. Stephen had insisted that he should spend his Christmas with them. And, in brief, there he was. He had walked from Bursley. Stephen, kept by business, was coming later, and so was some of the baggage.

Mr Bittenger's face radiated joy. The loss of his twenty-guinea passage on the *Saxonia* did not appear to cause him the least regret.

And he sat down by the side of Vera.

And Vera suddenly noticed that they were on a sofa – the sofa of her dream – and she fancied she recognized the room.

'You know, my dear lady,' said Mr Bittenger, looking her straight in the eyes, 'I'm just *glad* I missed my steamer. It gives me the chance to spend a Christmas in England, and in your delightful society – your delightful society——' He gazed at her, without adding to the sentence.

If this was not love-making on a sofa, what could be?

Mr Bittenger had certainly missed the Liverpool express on purpose. Of that Vera was convinced. Or, if he had not missed it on purpose, he had missed it under the dictates of the mysterious power of the dream. Those people who chose to believe that dreams are nonsense were at liberty to do so.

IV

So that in spite of Vera's definite proclamation that there should be no Christmassing in her house that year, Christmassing there emphatically was. Impossible to deny anything to Mr Bittenger! Mr Bittenger wanted holly, the gardener supplied it. Mr Bittenger wanted mistletoe, a bunch of it was brought home by Stephen in the dogcart. Mr Bittenger could not conceive an English Christmas without turkey, mince-pies, plum-pudding, and all the usual indigestiveness. Vera, speaking in a voice which seemed somehow not to be hers, stated that these necessaries of Christmas life would be produced, and Stephen did not say that the very thought of a mince-tart made him ill. Even the English weather, which, it is notorious, has of late shown a sad disposition to imitate, and even to surpass, in mildness the weather of the Riviera at Christmas, decided to oblige Mr Bittenger. At nightfall on Christmas Eve it began to snow gently, but steadily – fine, frozen snow. And the waits, consisting of boys and girls from the Countess of Chell's celebrated institute close by, came and sang in the garden in the falling snow, by the light of a lantern. And Mr Bittenger's heart was as full as it could hold of English Christmas.

As for Vera's heart, it was full of she knew not what. Mr Bittenger's attitude towards her grew more and more chivalrous. He contrived to indicate that he regarded all the years he had spent before making the acquaintance of Vera as so many years absolutely wasted. And Stephen did not seem to care.

They retired to rest that evening up a staircase whose banisters the industrious hands of Mr Bittenger had entwined with holly and paper festoons, and bade each other good-night, and wished each other a merry Christmas with immense fervour; but in the conjugal chamber Stephen maintained his policy of implacable silence. And, naturally, Vera maintained hers. Could it be expected of her that she should yield? The fault was all Stephen's. He ought to have taken her to The Bear, Switzerland. Then there would have been no dream, no Mr Bittenger, and no danger. But as things were, within twenty-four hours he would be a dead man.

And throughout Christmas Day Vera, beneath the gaiety with which she met the vivacious sallies of Mr Bittenger, waited in horrible suspense for the dream to fulfil itself. Stephen alone observed her agitated condition. Stephen said to himself: 'The quarrel is getting on her nerves. She'll yield before she's a day older. It will do her good. Then I'll make it up to her handsomely. But she must yield first.'

He little knew that he was standing on the edge of the precipice of death.

The Christmas dinner succeeded admirably; and Stephen, in whom courage was seldom lacking, ate half a mince-pie. The day was almost over. No premature decease had so far occurred. And when both the men said that, if Vera permitted, they would come with her at once to the drawing-room and smoke there, Vera decided that after all dreams were nonsense. She entered the drawing-room first, and Mr Bittenger followed her, with Stephen behind; but just as Stephen was crossing the mat the gardener, holding a parcel in his hands and looking rather strange there in the hall, spoke to him. And Stephen stopped and called to Mr Bittenger. And the drawing-room door was closed upon Vera.

She waited, solitary, for an incredible space of time, and then, having heard unaccustomed and violent sounds in the

distance, she could contain herself no longer, and she rang the bell.

'Louisa,' she demanded of the parlourmaid, 'where is your master?'

'Oh, ma'am,' replied Louisa, giggling – a little licence was surely permissible to the girl on Christmas night – 'Oh, ma'am, there's such a to-do! Tinsley has just brought some boxing-gloves, and master and Mr Bittenger have got their coats off in the dining-room. And they've had the table pushed up by the door, and you never saw such a set-out in all your life, ma'am.'

Vera dismissed Louisa.

There it was – the dream! They were going to box. Mr Bittenger was doubtless an expert, and she knew that Stephen was not. A chance blow by Mr Bittenger in some vital part, and Stephen would be lying stretched in eternal stillness in the middle of the dining-room floor where the table ought to be! The life of the monster was at stake! The life of the brute was in her hands! The dream was fulfilling itself to the point of tragedy!

She jumped up and rushed to the dining-room door. It would not open. Again, the dream!

'You can't come in,' cried Stephen, laughing. 'Wait a bit.'

She pushed against the door, working the handle.

She was about to insist upon the door being opened, when the idea of the danger of such a proceeding occurred to her. In the dream, when she got the door opened, her husband's death had already happened!

Frantically she ran to the kitchen.

'Louisa,' she ordered. 'Go into the garden and tap at the dining-room window, and tell your master that I must speak to him at once in the drawing-room.'

And in a pitiable state of excitation, she returned to the drawing-room.

After another interminable period of suspense, her ear

caught the sound of the opening of doors, and then Stephen came into the drawing-room. A singular apparition! He was coatless, as Louisa had said, and the extremities of his long arms were bulged out with cream-coloured boxing-gloves.

She sprang at him and kissed him.

'Steve,' she said, 'are we friends?'

'I should think we were!' he replied, returning her kiss heartily. He had won.

'What are you doing?' she asked him.

'Bittenger and I are just going to have a real round with the gloves. It's part of his cure for my indigestion, you know. He says there's nothing like it. I've only just been able to get the gloves. Tinsley brought them up just now. And so we sort of thought we'd like to have a go at once.'

'Why wouldn't you let me into the dining-room?'

'My child, the table was up against the door. And I fancied, perhaps, you wouldn't be exactly charmed, so I——'

'Stephen,' she said, in her most persuasive voice, 'will you do something to please me?'

'What is it?'

'Will you?'

A pause.

'Yes, certainly.'

'Don't box to-night.'

'Oh – well! What will Bittenger think?'

Another pause.

'Never mind! You don't want me to box, really?'

'I don't want you to box – not to-night.'

'Agreed, my chuck!' And he kissed her again. He could well afford to be magnanimous.

Mr Bittenger ploughed the seas alone to New York.

But supposing that Vera had not interfered, what would have happened? That is the unanswerable query which torments the superstitious little brain of Vera.

Christmas 1656

ELIAS ASHMOLE

*The famous antiquary who was Lichfield born and educated
always maintained a connection with his native city which he
presented with a loving cup. The Mrs Dugdale referred to was
the wife of his friend, Sir William Dugdale, the Warwickshire
antiquary whose daughter would become Ashmole's third wife.
His fellow Staffordshire historian Dr Robert Plot became the first
curator of the Ashmolean Museum.*

19 Dec. 1656
I went toward Blyth hall.

After Christmas, 1656
Being entertain'd at Blyth Hall, the Christmas 1656. I sent
these Verses to Mrs: Dugdale after my first daies Journey
thence:

> The longest Day at length resignes its Light,
> To'th conquering shade of the approaching night:
> The stately Oak (though arm'd with knotty crust
> As proof 'gainst ruine) stoops & falls to dust:
> All Men & things, like to the fleeting Sun,
> No sooner rise but to their setting run,
> Thus iolly Christmas droopes, and's welneere spent,
> And with it that Felicity it lent.
> Yet while he tarried, with a pleas'd delight

My Soule on quiet fed, my Appetite
On such brave Vyands, as the daies of yore
Furnisht our Gentry with, from their owne store,
To make old Hospitality look high,
Adding their Nut-browne Ale & History.

'Twas at your house I saw the Face & State
Of aged Christmas, (with most, out of date)
Where Holly, Joy, sacred Mistletoe,
His ancient Cognizance & Liv'ry show,
Where, in the Brawne, Plumbroth, & minc't Pies,
Nor Superstition nor Prophaness lies,
Where every thing such solemne order wore,
As holy Festivalls did heretofore,
And where (to crowne the whole) your hearty cleere,
And cheerfull lookes exceeded all the Cheere.

But stay; me thinks the Jollity that whet
Our heavy Spleenes, I should not heere forget;
The reveren'd Bag-Piper, whose Hymns & Sonnets,
Smelt rank of Robyn Wisdome, & Scotch Bonnets,
And skilfull Judd that exercisd his Tabour
As't would haue freed the Moone out of her Labour;
The Mask of Mummors, who the patient Roome
O're charged with the strength of their perfume:
The active Yule-games, & the trecherous bump
That my assistance lent the Young mans Rump,
And last of all, the Possit without Milk
(Is not the Cook worth's weight in burned Silk?)
But now all these are vanisht, with the Howres,
That brought them forth; Thus Tyme our Joy devours.

And yet Alas! Tis not the loss of Bliss,
(But giving Torments heere) that Torment is;

The churlish Nurse, who to her Babe denyes
The Brest, & Mustard adds; this wets it's Eyes.
Is't not enough that thus I banisht be,
From all that's good, but must be forc'd to flee
Just when the Storme impetuous growes & when
Aeolus has loos'd his Prisnors from their den.
Sad Fate! Nay sadder yet, cause I must goe
(Through all these Stormes) to meete uncertaine woe.

Yet heer's my hope, when next I visit you,
These Ills will vanish with that Morning's Dew.

from

Correspondence of Josiah Wedgwood

*The great potter maintained a correspondence with the Lichfield
literary circle including Dr Erasmus Darwin and Anna
Seward. This letter of 1786 contains a balance between
the scientific interest and the social niceties of the
festive season.*

To Dr Darwin

ETRURIA, *27 Decr. 86*

My Dear Sir,

Mr Kirwan has just published the inclosed *Estimate of the temperature of different latitudes*, & begs your acceptance of this copy.

I told Mr K. that you had some clever thoughts about the origin & course of winds, but I did not know that you intended to make them public. He wished you would, & was very glad you had turned your attention to meteorological subjects. He

Etruria Hall

144

has collected many facts he says upon the motion of the atmosphere, & will gladly put them into your hands, as he does not mean to persue the wind himself. Pray write a line to him. I almost promised him you would, & it will come in so pat & clever when you thank him for his excellent temperature that I think you cannot avoid it.

All here wish your mince pies & plum puddings sweet & well seasoned, & seasonable appetites for the rencontres. Susan is going to Morton in the morning, & will take your Xmass complimts with her if you please. Ours ever wait upon the Darwinians great & small & – & – what can I say more, but that I am most sincerely yours

J.W.

from

Dyott's Diary

As the second son of a landed family William Dyott pursued an army career which took him to Nova Scotia, the West Indies, Egypt, and Ireland. On the death of his brother he inherited the Freeford estate where he then adapted to the life of a county landowner. His diary, 1781–1845, reflected the concerns of his class particularly during the passage of the 1832 Reform Bill but obviously he saw Christmas as a time for the family.

1831

December 25th. – Christmas Day. I had hopes to have collected all my dear children round my table on this day, but was disappointed. Dick could not obtain leave, and his unfortunate wretched brother's extraordinary conduct, continuing to prevail to the exclusion of his presence at Freeford, I had only my beloved Eleanor to accompany me in paying our humble obedience to Divine Providence on this holy day. My sister Mary came to us as usual to pass her Christmas.

1832

January. – I commence another year with the most devout and heartfelt gratitude for the blessings of the past, and if I should have a continuance for the year that is to come of the health I have enjoyed, it will be the utmost hope of the protection of an all-ruling and Divine Providence.

Fine open weather until the 4th. Sharp frost.

December. – On the 18th Miss Bakewell arrived to pass the Christmas.

23rd, Sunday. – The rain was so continual, we could not get to Church; a circumstance that does not occur more than once in a month.

Farewell 1832; a year replete with many extraordinary publick events; memorable for England for the great change effected in the British Constitution by the enactment of the reform bill, whether propitious or otherwise as affecting the country generally, time only can determine. The passing events of the year pretty clearly demonstrate the power and influence the great mass of the *people* have assumed, and practised; betokening the democratick feeling to prevail to an extent much to be feared as leading to revolt, or perhaps something worse. The general elections, particularly in the composition of the house is considered, and the momentous affairs that must occupy its attention.

1833

January 1. – I am now commencing another year of my pilgrimage in this world. How transitory and uncertain are all the ways of Divine Providence, and how truly thankful ought we to feel for the manifold blessings we enjoy.

1835

December 20th. – Extremely cold with sleet and snow. I walked to church. My dear Eleanor was prevented attending by the weather.

Very sharp frost continued until the 27th. On Xmas Day we attended divine service, and received the Holy Sacrament after a good discourse from the Rev. T. Levett. My sister Mary returned in the carriage with Miss Bakewell and Eleanor to pass the Xmas. Lord Anglesey wanted me to pay him a visit during the week, but as he mentioned the large party he had in the house, I made my excuse by telling him that my unfortunate deafness precluded any enjoyment of large parties. He said if I could *hear*, I should be delighted with a man staying in the house, Lord Alvanley, one of the most entertaining men of the day. It did not tempt me.

1836

December 25th – Christmas Day. Snow in the morning and deep snow in the course of the day. We attended Divine Service and Sacrament, and for (I believe) the first time in my life, I went in the carriage. I had been mostly confined to the house during the week, and with the ground covered with snow I was afraid to attempt my weekly walk. I have been looking out for the past two days for my dear Dick. My hopes are disappointed by not having him to pass Christmas Day at home. The Mediterranean Packet is, I think, due on the 25th. I look forward with anxiety for New Year's Day in the hope of having all my dear children at my table on that day. In the course of Christmas night, a tremendous blow, with a heavy fall of snow, causing unusual drifts.

There was no Christmas mail for General Dyott in 1836 but nearly 150 years later these local postladies braved the elements – Barbara Neal

148

delivered Stonnall's mail by sledge while Gladys Smith managed the bike
at Hamstall Ridware

No mail arrived at Lichfield on the 26th or 27th, a complete stoppage having taken place at Chalk Hill near Dunstable, again near Dunchurch and near Welford. Communication was cut off in all directions for two days, 26th and 27th, with hard blowing weather and continued snow.

1837

January 1, Sunday. – New Year's Day.
2nd. – Miss Bakewell left us. I sent my horses to convey her to Stapenhill on a visit to Mrs Abney, calling in her way at Drakelow. My horses did not return until seven o'clock in the evening. I and Eleanor did not lament the loss of our guest. She is the most accomplished tiresome being that nature ever manufactured. My poor Eleanor had more of her plague and torment than I had. Indeed I would not have supported *ten* hours a day of such a repetition of plague and pestilence.

1844

December 25th. – I went to church and received the Holy Sacrament with my two dear children. My dear Bill after the performance of his duty to his parishioners at the Vicarage came home to dinner to join our Christmas party with my brother Phillip. There was the usual entertainment in the servants' hall of roast beef and plum pudding, and I hope no lack of jollity and Christmas festivity.

1845

January 1, Wednesday. – It pleased Almighty Providence to allow me to commence another year in this world. For although the decay of old age has naturally occasioned aches and pains, I have grateful feelings for the blessings of the year now passed.

Acknowledgements

The extract from *Daisy's Lichfield* is reproduced by kind permission of the author, Daisy Winder, and her publisher, J.M. Sanders of Lichfield. 'Winter Wonderland' by Phil Drabble is from *Country Wise*, published by Michael Joseph Ltd and is reproduced by kind permission of the author. 'Wassail Time' by J.E. Roberts is from *Bilberry Pie* and is reproduced by kind permission of Mrs Dora Roberts. 'Christmas Letter to Father' by David Garrick is reprinted by permission of the publishers from *The Letters of David Garrick*, edited by David M. Little and George M. Kahrl, Cambridge, Mass.: The Belknap Press of Harvard University Press, Copyright © 1963 by the President and Fellows of Harvard College. The 'Scruts' parody from *A Christmas Garland* by Sir Max Beerbohm is reproduced by permission of the copyright owner, Mrs Eva Reichmann. The extract from *Testament of Youth* by Vera Brittain is included with the permission of Paul Berry, her literary executor, and Victor Gollancz Ltd. 'Christmas 1656' from *Elias Ashmole 1617–1692* by C.H. Josten, volume II, 1966, is reproduced by permission of Oxford University Press.

The compiler would like to express his thanks to staff at Birmingham, Cannock, Hanley, and William Salt libraries and the Lichfield Record Office for all their help and advice.

Picture Credits

Pages viii, 7, 11, 30, 32, 36, 53, 64, 73, 76, 88, 148, 149 – *Lichfield Mercury* (Allan Williamson). 3, 70 – from *Around Rugeley in Old Photographs* by Thea Randall and Joan Anslow. 16, 94, 128 – William Salt Library, Stafford. 19, 67 – E.J.D. Warrillow collection, Keele University Library. 39, 46, 49, 62 – Cannock Library. 43, 112, 132 – from *Around Cannock in Old Photographs* by Mary Mills and Sherry Belcher. 85, 101, 135 – Hanley Library. 103 – from *Around Stafford in Old Photographs* by Joan Anslow and Thea Randall. 108 – Shugborough Hall (Marketing and Publicity). The *In Old Photographs* series is published by Alan Sutton Publishing.